HOW TO THINK LIKE A PSYCHOLOGIST

Critical Thinking in Psychology

Donald H. McBurney

University of Pittsburgh

Prentice Hall
Upper Saddle River, New Jersey 07458

Library of Congress Cataloging-in-Publication Data

McBurney, Donald,
   How to think like a psychologist: critical thinking in psychology
   /Donald H. McBurney.
      p.   cm.
   Includes bibliographical references.
   ISBN 0-02-378392-3
   1. Psychology. 2. Critical thinking. I. Title.
   BF38.5M445 1996
   150--dc20   95-25246
                                                              CIP

Editorial/production supervision: *Harriet Tellem*
Acquisitions editor: *Peter Janzow*
Editorial assistant: *Marilyn Coco*
Manufacturing buyer: *Tricia Kenny*
Cover designer: *Bruce Kenselaar*

 © 1996 by Prentice-Hall, Inc.
Simon & Schuster/A Viacom Company
Upper Saddle River, New Jersey 07458

Printed in the United States of America

10 9   8   7   6   5   4   3   2

ISBN   0-02-378392-3

Prentice-Hall International (UK) Limited, *London*
Prentice-Hall of Australia Pty. Limited, *Sydney*
Prentice-Hall Canada Inc., *Toronto*
Prentice-Hall Hispanoamericana, S.A., *Mexico*
Prentice-Hall of India Private Limited, *New Delhi*
Prentice-Hall of Japan, Inc., *Tokyo*
Simon & Schuster Asia Pte. Ltd., *Singapore*
Editora Prentice-Hall do Brasil, Ltda., *Rio de Janeiro*

Contents

BIOLOGICAL BASES

DEVELOPMENT

SENSATION/PERCEPTION

CONSCIOUSNESS

LEARNING AND MEMORY

THINKING AND LANGUAGE

MOTIVATION AND EMOTION

PSYCHOLOGICAL TESTING AND INTELLIGENCE

PERSONALITY AND ABNORMAL PSYCHOLOGY

SOCIAL PSYCHOLOGY

Preface

Too often, students find the content and methods of their introductory psychology course to be very different from what they expected. Partly this is because few of them have studied psychology in high school, but the ones who have seem equally alienated by the course, if not more so. After teaching introductory psychology for more than thirty years, I have come to realize that students have many misconceptions about science, and psychology in particular, that serve as impediments to understanding psychology.

As a consequence of this realization, I spend much of the class time dealing with these misconceptions. One mechanism for doing this is to have students turn in written questions at the beginning of class for me to answer. This excuse gives me the opportunity to deal with some issues that may seem peripheral to the course but pose significant stumbling blocks to understanding what we think of as the material of the course.

This book answers some of the most common questions asked by my students. By so doing, it seeks to motivate students by dealing directly with their real concerns. The answers to their questions illuminate principles of psychology and philosophy of science that present stumbling blocks to students' understanding of psychology.

Another stimulus for this book comes from the current interest in teaching critical thinking skills. Too many books, and too many students, appear to treat science in general, and introductory science courses in particular, as a collection of facts to be mastered for an exam. To be sure, one of the essential tasks of an introductory psychology course is to introduce students to a wide variety of technical terms, research paradigms, and empirical data. But the main goal of a psychology course should be to get students to think like psychologists; to apply the same critical skills to human behavior that scientists do.

Critical thinking is a very large umbrella for a number of skills and attitudes that educators attempt to instill in their students (e.g., Brookfield, 1987). Instructors have had these same goals from time immemorial. Recently, however, research in cognitive psychology applied to the learning process (Resnick, 1987) demonstrates two principles that are significant to teaching critical thinking in psychology: (1) Critical thinking is not learned in the abstract, but in the specific subject matters of the various disciplines, and (2) the skills needed for critical thinking vary from discipline to discipline:

> One cannot reason in the abstract; one must reason about something....Each discipline has characteristic ways of thinking and reasoning....Reasoning and problem solving in the physical sciences, for example, are shaped by particular combinations of inductive and deductive reasoning, by appeal to mathematical tests, and by an extensive body of agreed upon fact for which new theories must account. In the social sciences, good reasoning and problem solving are much more heavily influenced by traditions of rhetorical argument, of weighing alternatives, and of "building a case" for a proposed solution....Only if higher order skills are taught within each discipline are they likely to be learned. (p. 36)

I believe that the answers to the questions posed in this book provide a highly motivating way to help students develop the skills necessary to think like psychologists.

This book takes a different approach to critical thinking than most others do. The principles covered do not map especially well onto the list of skills generally promulgated as characterizing critical thinking, which tends to be less domain specific. Rather, the book models the process of critical thinking and encourages the student to engage in it. John McPeck (1990) says:

> I think that the phrase "critical thinking" refers to a certain *combination* of what we might think of as a willingness, or disposition (call it an "attitude," if you like), together with the appropriate knowledge and skills, to engage in an activity or problem with *reflective skepticism*. (p. 42) (emphasis in the original)

The attitude of reflective skepticism is one that is insufficiently encouraged in our educational system, for reasons that I discuss in the introduction to this book.

The book takes strong positions on certain controversial issues, such as the paranormal. I believe that the principles stated and positions taken are well within the mainstream of academic, research-based psychology. Thus, the book should be compatible with the viewpoints of the typical introductory psychology text and instructors of psychology courses.

Psychology, however, is a heterogeneous field, and I do not pretend to reflect all points of view, some of which are mutually contradictory.

I try to strike a balance between critical thinking and open-mindedness. Paul and Nosich (1991) list the following as part of critical thinking: "fairmindedness, intellectual humility...willingness to see objections, enter sympathetically into another's point of view, [and] to recognize one's own egocentricity or ethnocentricity" (p. 5). Even when I inevitably fail to meet these ideals, it is my experience that students appreciate finding out where I stand on an issue. They are sophisticated enough not to swallow whole what I say.

The book attempts to represent the common philosophical tradition within which psychologists work. I have not, in general, tried to reflect the latest developments in philosophy of science. This is a book for beginners in psychology; I leave the finer points to later study.

The organization of the topics is designed to follow the most common order of chapters in an introductory psychology book. The material could be assigned along with the text and dealt with in class or in recitation sections. Exercises at the end of each section invite the reader to apply the principle just discussed. The book is intended also to be helpful for students of research methods, history and systems, and other later courses in psychology.

A number of people have contributed to the development of this book. Robert D. Jewell, University of Calgary; Jane F. Gaultney, University of North Carolina, Charlotte; Tony Johnson, LaGrange College; John T. Long, Mt. San Antonio College; Drew Appleby, Marion College; and Bruce Goldstein, University of Pittsburgh; made helpful comments on the manuscript. I have tried to acknowledge the sources of ideas when possible. I have absorbed many of the points, and even some of the examples and phrases, from others over the years, and the sources have been forgotten. My apologies to any who should have been cited.

Donald H. McBurney

Introduction

What Is Critical Thinking?

Cutter Emerick was my fifth grade social studies teacher. He was fascinating to his students not only because of his unusual first name, but also for his curly hair that he carefully tried to comb over his bald spot. Unfortunately, when the weather was humid, his hair would roll up into a tight curl and leave his head bare. One day I asked him in class why his hair sometimes curled up and showed his bald spot. He showed a distinct lack of interest in this question. When I asked my father about this curious phenomenon, he said the humidity caused Mr. Emerick's hair to curl up. The next day I said in class that I knew why his hair curled up. Mr. Emerick was not pleased.

Perhaps it was this incident; perhaps it was because I corrected him publicly when he told the class that Niagara Falls faced the United States; perhaps it was because I was always asking questions in class. But one day he finally lost his temper when I asked one question too many.

My father, on the other hand, would answer any question I asked in as much detail as I wanted. (Well, almost any. When I asked him how the rooster managed to copulate with the hens when he didn't have the kind of male parts other barnyard animals have, he mumbled something I couldn't make out.) Later, when my own kids entered the why stage, I asked my father how long it would last. He said, "Forever, if you're lucky." Most people, however, outgrow the why stage. Some of those who don't outgrow it become psychologists.

So when I began to hear more and more about something new called critical thinking, I felt like the character in Molière who was surprised to learn that he had been speaking prose all his life without knowing it. I had been doing critical thinking since I was a little kid and teaching critical thinking as an integral feature of my courses all along.

What is critical thinking? As popular as this concept is, there seems to be little agreement about its definition. I believe that critical thinking is primarily an attitude of asking why—why is that so; why did that happen; why should I believe that claim? Unfortunately, most kids have at least one Mr. Emerick for a teacher. They learn that it is easier not to ask questions.

Long after I was a professor, I took some additional graduate courses in another school at my university. One instructor was very explicit about his desire that we understand his material and that we ask questions when things were not clear. He would stop lecturing every few minutes and say, "Is that clear—Susan?" Every student in the class would always say "yes," including me. The problem was, the material was often unclear to me. One day when he said, "Don, is that clear?" I stiffened my resolve and said, "No." The entire class looked at me as if I had make a rude noise. Later, during the break, several thanked me and said that they never understood what he was talking about. So a whole web of experiences, habits, social expectations, instructors' body language, and the like work against the application of critical thinking. We learn that there are the rules, and there are the real rules. We have years of training in passivity before we get to college. You can get into trouble by doing critical thinking, as many a small child with more curiosity than social grace has found out.

How does one teach critical thinking? Years ago, educators emphasized general principles of thinking that could be applied to any area of study. This was part of the reason so many of us studied Latin in high school. Today, however, there is broad agreement that critical thinking skills are best learned in the context of a particular discipline rather than in the abstract. Cognitive psychologists have found that in order to think like an expert in a discipline, one must have a considerable base of knowledge in that discipline. Further, critical thinking skills learned in one discipline do not always transfer to another.

For these reasons, I will avoid giving lists of rules for critical thinking, as if one could simply memorize them and then be a critical thinker. This is as impossible as becoming an expert pianist by memorizing the keys on the piano. Instead, we will take up a number of typical questions that students have asked me over the years that reveal stumbling blocks to understanding psychology. The answers to each of these questions involve the application of a particular principle or critical thinking skill that is important in psychology. It is my hope that studying these principles and exercising these skills will help you begin to think like a psychologist.

Section 1

Why Do Psychologists Use So Much Jargon?

Principle: *Terms are used in science in a technical sense that is often very different from the everyday sense of the term.*

Specialists frequently annoy us by using their own arcane vocabulary. Why is it necessary to say *learning resources center* instead of *library,* or *sanitation engineer* instead of *garbage collector?* Why do psychologists talk about *negative reinforcement* instead of *punishment?*

The word *jargon* has two meanings of interest to us. The first meaning refers to an obscure, pretentious language characterized by the use of fancy words—and usually more of them than necessary. I do not defend the use of jargon in this sense. People who use jargon this way are trying either to sound important, or to snow the listener, or both. They wind up sounding pompous and boring instead.

The second meaning of the word *jargon* is technical language characteristic of a specialized group. Any specialty, whether scientific, artistic, or whatever, requires some special language. In sailing, *coming about* refers to the maneuver of changing direction in such a way that the boat, which has been sailing at an angle toward the direction from which the wind is blowing, turns directly toward the wind but continues to turn so that the wind is now blowing at an angle onto the other side of the boat. (I purposely avoided using any technical sailing terms to describe the process of coming about.)

When the skipper says, "Ready about," these two words tell the crew exactly what he wants to happen and what they are required to do to accomplish it. It might seem more understandable to a novice if the skipper said, "Get ready to turn," but an experienced crew would be in the dark about what they should do next. The jargon saves a great deal of time and effort by conveying precise and often complicated information in a concise form.

Jargon always makes it hard for outsiders to understand what some group of specialists is talking about, but the good use of jargon improves communication among knowledgeable people. The problem is how to decide whether a particular example is technical in the proper sense or whether it is just pretentious. Most of us might agree that *sanitation engineer* is jargon in the bad sense, because it is mainly used in an effort to make the occupation sound more high class than *garbage collector*. The case of the learning resources center is not so clear. Those who like this term will say that it conveys the notion that the center contains not just books, but also films, audio and video material, and the like. But probably everyone knows that already, in which case the term *library* would do just fine. In the case of sailing, however, knowing all the technical terms for the parts of a boat and the actions taken in sailing can not only save much effort and confusion, it can also even be a matter of life and death.

Psychologists use their share of jargon. For example, we distinguish between the terms *punishment* and *negative reinforcement*. The first term may sound like ordinary English, and the second may sound like jargon. Laypeople often use the two interchangeably, assuming negative reinforcement is just a fancy way of saying punishment. In fact, they are very different.

Punishment refers to an unpleasant event that is *presented* when someone does something. A child may be spanked for stealing a cookie, for example. Negative reinforcement, however, refers to an unpleasant experience that is *removed* when someone does something. A child may be permitted to come out of her room after she apologizes to her brother for calling him a name. The important distinction is that punishment always *reduces or eliminates* some behavior, such as stealing cookies, whereas negative reinforcement, like any other reinforcement, *increases* the frequency of some behavior, such as apologizing. Failure to distinguish between the two terms leads to a failure to understand the difference between two psychological processes.

Even when scientists do not seem to be using jargon, they may be. Scientists often use words that originally came from everyday usage, but they have given these different definitions when they use them scientifically. We have already used the example of punishment. This term came from everyday usage, but it has been given a specific definition that is not the same as the everyday definition you would find in a dictionary. This practice can also be frustrating to laypeople.

I remember attending a conference on olfaction (jargon for the sense of smell) in which we spent a long time trying to define odor. The spouse of one of the conferees, who had sat in on the meeting, said afterward with some exasperation, "Why didn't you just look in the dictionary and be done with it?" The reason we didn't was that the dictionary definition is not intended to deal with the distinctions that scientists need to make when dealing with odor.

The simplest example may be how the term *work* is used in physics. We know in everyday life that work can consist of many different activities, some of which are purely mental, as when we work on a problem in our head. But to the physicist, work is defined as force times distance. By the physicist's definition, if you stood for 10 minutes holding up a piece of lumber while someone else nailed it in place, you would have done no work because, although you exerted force, you did not move anything. By everyone else's definition, you would have done work, and hard work at that.

In psychology, students often think they understand what is being talked about because terms such as *reinforcement, punishment, discrimination,* and the like are being used. What they may be missing is that even though these terms sound like ordinary English, they are really a different language, with different definitions.

Exercise: Find three terms in the glossary of a psychology textbook that have everyday meanings that are different from their technical meanings.

Section 2

Why Don't You Skip the Theories and Give Us More Facts?

Principle: *The main goal of science is theories, not facts.*

People like facts. They seem direct and concrete. Theories, on the other hand, seem tentative and speculative. The line made famous by Sergeant Friday in *Dragnet* was, "Give me the facts, Ma'am, just the facts." Psychologists, on the other hand, always seem to be talking about theories: Pavlov's theory of conditioning, Freud's theory of the unconscious, and so on. Some of these theories contradict one another. As a result, students get the idea that nothing in psychology is known for sure and that we develop theories because we are unsure of the facts.

As a matter of fact (!), theories are far more important to science than facts. A *theory* is a set of interrelated concepts that explains a large number of facts in a particular area of study. Pavlov's theory of conditioning explains why dogs salivate to a bell after the ringing of the bell has been paired with the appearance of a little food in the dog's mouth. Pavlov developed his theory to explain why the dog salivated when the bell was rung without any food. Pavlov's theory is an explanation of the facts.

Science differs from most other human activities in that its primary goal is the understanding of a set of phenomena, not simply being able to predict or control them. An animal trainer may know a great deal of practical information about how to get a dog to jump through a hoop. In fact, most animal trainers certainly know far more about how to train a dog than almost any psychologist who does not happen to be an animal trainer as well. The goal of the animal trainer is to get the animal to jump through the hoop. The goal of the psychologist is to develop a theory to explain the processes that are involved when the dog learns to jump through the hoop.

The goal of the animal trainer is practical. The goal of the scientist is understanding. This is the difference between a cook and a chemist, an electrician and a physicist, a physician and a physiologist, an engineer and a scientist. My inclusion of the last two pairs of professions may require some elaboration in order to make the point clear. The physician and the engineer study a lot of science in their training. And physicians and engineers may both at times be involved in scientific research. But the goal of the physician is healing people, whereas the goal of engineers is building a rocket, or whatever. The practical and scientific roles of some professions overlap enough that we often talk of science and engineering as a single category for purposes of education, employment, and the like. Nevertheless, it is necessary to understand that generally the scientist is the only one whose main goal is to develop an understanding of whatever it is she is working on.

You might object that both the scientist and the practitioner have the goal of understanding. But the goal of the practitioner is recipe knowledge: practical, or "how to," knowledge. The goal of the scientist is theoretical, or "why," knowledge. Once, when I was teaching about personality theory in introductory psychology, a student offered to bring in some very good films from her place of business that she thought would be helpful in studying personality. Upon questioning her, I discovered that the films were training films on how to get along better with fellow employees, how to be a better manager of people, and similar topics. No doubt these were excellent films, and very helpful to her company and its employees. But they were aimed at imparting "how to" knowledge, not theoretical knowledge.

There are many reasons why scientists are so interested in theory. A good theory will explain facts that previously were not seen to be related; it will suggest further research that results in new facts; it will suggest new ways of dealing with problems that people face. Someone has said that nothing is as practical as a good theory. Theoretical understanding of learning has improved animal training as well as classroom instruction; theoretical understanding of disease processes has led to new treatments for disease, and so on.

But you are probably still bothered by my emphasis on the importance of theories. Don't we ever get to the point where we prove a theory to be a fact? Actually, a theory that is accepted by all as true is still a theory. We still talk about the germ theory of disease, or the gene theory of heredity, or Einstein's theory of relativity, even though there is no serious doubt that they are all true.

Once when I was trying to explain this to a class, one of the students asked, "Do you mean that a theory never grows up to become a fact?" The student had gotten the point. Some theories are wrong; some theories are better supported than others. But a theory cannot grow up to be anything else, because there is nothing better to become.

This last point is misunderstood by religious fundamentalists who claim that creationism should be taught in schools along with evolution because Darwin's theory is only a theory. Now evolution is a "fact" because it happened. (In other words, the theory of evolution is true, because it explains a great many facts.) But it is still a theory, because it is an explanation (the only scientific one, in fact) of a (very large) set of observations.

> **Exercise:** Name several theories of science that are "facts" in the everyday sense, because they are universally accepted as true.

Section 3

But That's Just Your Theory!

Principle: *Scientists as a rule believe the theory that gives the best explanation of a phenomenon, not just the one they like best.*

Occasionally when I am lecturing about some topic and I describe the theory behind it, a student will say, "But that's just your theory; mine is such and such." More often, they sit there and write down what I say so they can regurgitate it for the test, and keep on believing what they want.

Students sometimes have the attitude that they should decide to accept a theory because it appeals to them more than others. Never mind that the theory I am describing is the one accepted by most psychologists. Never mind that it is supported by empirical evidence. Never mind that it makes connections with related theories in other areas of science.

This is a tricky problem to deal with. It is true that no theory explains everything there is to know about a topic. It is true that all theories are incomplete explanations, or oversimplifications, of reality. It is true that there are often competing theories for any given phenomenon, and that each one will explain certain facts better than the other. So most scientists will not claim that any particular theory is 100% correct.

It is also true that there is plenty of evidence that scientists let their biases influence how they decide which theory to prefer. Many times a scientist will prefer one theory to another because it seems more aesthetically pleasing.

An influential movement in the humanities, known as *postmodernism,* questions whether it is possible to discover truth independent of personal biases, assumptions, viewpoints, and the like. A number of social psychologists (for example, Gergen, 1994) have argued that psychology has much to learn from postmodernism.

As an example of how biases can influence scientists, consider sexual behavior. Scientists used to assume that the male rat was the more active partner in initiating and timing of sexual behavior. More recently it has been found that the female actually controls the situation. It has become appreciated that the female of most species tends to be the more choosy sex and thus plays a large role in the timing of sexual encounters.

The idea that bias and personal preference causes us to prefer one theory over another is compatible with postmodernism. Thus we have feminist psychology, Marxist psychology, existential psychology, and so forth. Postmodernists, for their part, say that mainstream psychology makes assumptions that are just as biased as those of, say, Marxist psychology.

Now the issue of postmodernism is a very complicated one, and I am not prepared to reject it completely. But most psychologists would agree that, whatever our biases are, there is only one reality, and the goal of science is to develop theories that best describe that reality. Our biases will get in the way of discovering that reality, to be sure, but empirical methods will eventually bring us closer to finding out the nature of the world.

So when your professor is expounding a theory to explain some phenomenon, she or he most likely believes that the theory best accounts for actual empirical evidence that relates to the phenomenon. It isn't just the one that he or she likes best for personal, aesthetic, political, religious, or whatever, reason.

Exercise: Ask your instructor if he or she has presented a theory to you because it is the one generally accepted while he or she actually prefers another one. Ask for the instructor's reasons for preferring the other theory.

Section 4

You're So Logical!

Principle: *It's pretty hard to be correct when your logic is wrong.*

As Dave Barry says, I am not making this up, although it is second-hand. A professor was having a vigorous discussion with a colleague about some theoretical question. When the colleague was cornered by his reasoning, he replied in exasperation, "You're so logical! I'm not sure I believe in logic!"

Now we all get frustrated when someone is always one jump ahead of us in an argument. But this person was saying that he knew he was right, regardless of whether it was logical or not. His attitude is actually a fairly widespread one, even among academicians, and has deep roots in the Romantic movement of the eighteenth and nineteenth Centuries.

The Romantics believed that rational thought and empirical evidence, the twin pillars of science, were unreliable because they overlooked direct knowledge based on human feelings (Hergenhahn, 1992). To the Romantic, science could never understand humans because it ignored those things that were most essentially human. The professor who said he wasn't sure he believed in logic was reflecting the Romantic movement's distrust of science.

Today many people feel alienated from science. They believe that science has served the forces of militarism, male domination, and ecological degradation that are such a large part of contemporary Western society. They blame science for the obvious imperfections of society, meanwhile taking for granted the health advances, computer games, and cellular phones that science has made possible (cf. Gross & Levitt, 1994).

11

I am not arguing that everything science has given us is wonderful. It should be obvious that no human institution is perfect. Nor am I saying that science is the only way we have of understanding ourselves. I enjoy literature, art, and theater as much as most people. I am simply arguing here that we should be very careful not to throw out the baby of science with the bathwater of mistakes made in the name of science.

Does admitting that science is not perfect justify a rejection of logical thought? Logical consistency is as essential to the success of science as it is in most human endeavors. A logical fallacy is no more or less devastating to science than it is to stamp collecting. (We do need to admit that there are areas of life, such as fashion, where logic plays little role. Prudence prevents me from listing others.)

The analysis of logical arguments is an involved, technical matter. We cannot do any more here than try to indicate how important it can be, both in everyday life and science. Take the matter of *logical fallacies*. These are arguments that tend to be persuasive even though they are faulty (Cederblom & Paulsen, 1986). One common logical fallacy is the *false dilemma*.

America: Love it or leave it.

This argument is evidently persuasive to some people because it was a popular bumper sticker slogan used against people who protested the Vietnam War. The reason it is fallacious is that other alternatives exist besides loving America just the way it is or emigrating. One can love one's own country and try to change it; one can love it and do nothing; one can love it and leave it, and so on.

Consider a hiker lost in the woods who comes to a fork in the trail. The marker has been vandalized and she has no basis for choosing one path over the other. She may stand there debating her alternatives, which seem to be limited to going left or right, especially if she is tired and hungry and not thinking clearly. But if she is a seasoned hiker, she may realize that staying put until someone rescues her may be the best alternative.

The false dilemma can be seen in scientific thinking. A scientist may want to design an experiment to choose between Smith's theory and Jones's. He thinks of a situation where the two theories make exactly opposite predictions. So far, so good. But then he decides that if the results come out one way, he will conclude that Smith's theory was correct; if it comes out the other, he will accept Jones's. The problem is that neither theory may be correct. In fact, even though the results lead you to reject, say, Smith's theory, you would not necessarily be correct in accepting Jones's. The experiment proved Smith's theory incorrect, but it was not designed in such a way to permit you to choose between Jones's theory and the true one that no one has yet thought of.

So when you are tempted to reject science because it seems too logical, or "linear," or "bourgeois," or "European," try to realize that logic is important to all human endeavors. We make logical errors at our peril no matter what we think of logic.

Exercise: Show why the following is an example of a false dilemma: If I don't cut up my credit cards, I'll never get them paid off.

Section 5

Why Do I Need to Learn All These Methods? I Just Want to Help People!

Principle: Professional practice of psychology benefits from an understanding of the scientific basis of practice.

At my university, like most, all psychology majors must take a course in research methods. This is not the most popular course I teach. Quite a number of students come right out and say, "Why do I need to learn all these methods? I just want to help people." They may agree that psychology should be based on scientific research. Why can't they just apply what scientific psychologists have found out and skip the research methods?

Psychology is distinctive among the human professions in the degree to which it requires its practitioners to study scientific methodology. The large majority of professional psychologists have earned a Ph.D. that required them to perform considerable amounts of research. This is not true of psychiatrists, social workers, and special educators. Psychology's emphasis on research is based on the idea that psychological practice is strengthened by a thorough understanding of psychological research methods.

An excellent example of the pitfalls of developing therapeutic techniques without sufficient research is given by the recent history of so-called *facilitated communication* (FC). This is a method used by thousands of special education teachers and speech therapists around the world to permit autistic persons to communicate by typing their thoughts on a computer terminal or similar keyboard. The facilitator holds the child's hand while the child supposedly chooses which letters to touch.

FC provided amazing and heartwarming examples whereby handicapped individuals apparently began communicating to their families and loved ones for the first time in their lives. Imagine the emotions experienced by a mother whose autistic child, previously completely uncommunicative, typed out, "I love you, Mom" on a computer. Syracuse University set up an Institute for Facilitated Communication, conferences were held, and FC became a worldwide movement.

The world of facilitated communication started to unravel when some autistic children, through FC, began accusing their parents of sexually molesting them. Their families suffered considerable anguish when they had to face expensive and protracted legal proceedings. One accused father had to stay away from home for months, during which he was not permitted any contact with his child.

Eventually Howard Shane of Boston Children's Hospital, an expert in developing means of communicating with the handicapped, was called in to investigate the claims of FC. He started out by arranging it so that the facilitator and the child saw different pictures, which the child was to describe by FC. For example, he showed a picture of a set of keys to the facilitator and one of a cup to the child. It became immediately evident that what was typed during FC was strictly what the facilitator saw, not what the child saw. In other words, the facilitator was typing what he or she saw or thought.

It must be emphasized that the facilitators were completely unaware that they were responsible for the movements of the child's hand. The realization of what they were doing was extremely distressing to the facilitators, and one of the leading proponents of FC refused to believe the evidence.

The simple test that was the undoing of FC is one that many first-year students of psychological research methods would think to do. But it had never been tried before, illustrating dramatically the need for training in research methods by those who work in the human services.

The FC fiasco is only one recent example of what has become known as the *Clever Hans effect*, after a horse that supposedly could read, write, and do arithmetic (including finding the factors of a number and adding fractions)—skills that college students sometimes have difficulty with. Hans created a sensation in the early 1900s in Germany and was tested by a zoologist, an animal behaviorist, a circus manager, a sensory physiologist, and a psychologist—all prominent in their fields.

Eventually a psychologist named Oskar Pfungst showed conclusively that Hans was responding not to the question asked him, but to extremely slight movements of the questioner's head, which signaled him to start or stop tapping the ground with his hoof. Like the FC facilitators, Hans's questioners were completely unaware of the movements they made that served as cues to Hans.

Of course, facilitated communication and Clever Hans were two aberrations in the history of psychology. Most psychological practice is firmly rooted in scientific research and works the way it is supposed to. But these examples illustrate why it is necessary for psychologists to know how to test the validity of psychological practices.

Exercise: Ask your instructor to describe the role that research played in his or her undergraduate and graduate training in psychology.

Section 6

But You've Taken All the Mystery Out of It!

Principle: *The goal of science is to solve puzzles, not to wonder at mysteries.*

Once when I was in college, I went to a humanities class straight from biology lab, smelling of formaldehyde. The professor asked me, "Why do biologists have to kill animals in order to study them? Biology is supposed to be the study of life!" Many people share the opinion of my humanities professor that scientists destroy what they try to study. They think we take the mystery out of it.

The truth is, we do. The term *mystery* is often used in the sense of a puzzle—we try to solve the mystery before the author reveals who the murderer was. But strictly speaking, mystery refers to something that we can't ever figure out; the answer has to be revealed to us by someone who knows, a prophet. A puzzle, on the other hand, is something that ordinary people can figure out.

Now everybody enjoys a mystery. We look at a flower, a baby, or a sunset and are struck with awe. But some people go into science expecting their study to contribute to this sense of wonder. Too many times, however, the wonder is blown away by a mass of decidedly unmysterious notions, and they decide to major in something else.

What these students are missing, however, is that science does not treat the world as a mystery, strictly speaking, but as a puzzle to be solved. A good example of the difference between a mystery and a puzzle is found in the motivations of those who study extrasensory perception (ESP).

In the early 1960s there was a great deal of interest in the claims that certain Russian women were able read with their fingertips. Because of the Cold War, it wasn't easy to find out what was going on in Russia. So when an American psychologist named Richard Youtz heard a report of an American woman who could tell colors with her fingers, he decided to study her. His experiments, which seemed to be well controlled, showed that she actually could tell colors with her fingertips.

Youtz reported his results at a meeting that I happened to attend. In fact, he gave his paper immediately before I was to deliver my first-ever scientific paper. The room was packed with hundreds of people for his talk. When he was done and it was my turn, the room emptied out except for about 20 people, which is the usual number who attend such talks.

A friend of mine named Walter Makous studies the senses. He wondered if there was some known ability of the skin that would make it possible to tell colors with the fingertips. He knew that the body gives off heat in the form of infrared radiation and that different colors reflect this heat back differentially. So he sat down and did some calculations that showed, on the basis of what was known about the temperature sensitivity of the skin and the reflectance of heat by colored objects, that it was theoretically possible for people to tell colors using the skin.

Then he did a simple experiment that showed that ordinary people could in fact do what he had found to be theoretically possible. He wrote up his findings in a major psychological journal.

What do you suppose was the result of his paper? Do you think that the ESPers rejoiced that the physiological basis of this extrasensory ability had been identified? The result was that interest in "dermo-optical perception" died completely and instantly.

The moral of this story is that people who study ESP are looking for a mystery—they are looking for something that *cannot* be explained. Scientists, on the other hand, try to find the answer to a puzzle. The difference is profound, as the story of dermo-optical perception indicates.

If you want a mystery, look at a flower, but don't take it apart; look at a baby, but don't ask questions that might have empirical answers. If you want a puzzle, go into science. There will be plenty of puzzles to solve, and you might even wind up deciding that there is some great mystery to the universe after all is said and done. Many scientists do find that their sense of mystery is actually increased by doing science. But when scientists do science, they are motivated by puzzles, not mysteries.

Exercise: How might considering child development as a puzzle to figure out, rather than a mystery to wonder at, lead one to take a different approach to working with children?

Exercise: Is someone who considers human behavior a puzzle rather than a mystery necessarily a killjoy?

Section 7

But This Contradicts Something I Believe

Principle: *Science contradicts everyone's beliefs, and that can be threatening for anyone.*

Students often get upset because something they learn in psychology contradicts some strongly held belief of theirs, or at least seems to. They may have been taught in Sunday school that we have free will, and the professor may teach that all behavior has a physical cause.

The relation between science and religion is a very large topic, and we cannot do justice to it here. Certainly some professors take some pleasure in challenging their students' religious beliefs. But the point here is a simple one. Science challenges *everyone's* beliefs, not just those of religious people. Being a scientist requires us to put our beliefs up to empirical test, to see if what we believe is in fact the case. And that is just as true whether the belief concerns free will or the mechanisms of memory.

So students who feel anxiety because something they learn challenges their view of the world are feeling exactly the same thing that every other person feels at one time or another. It may threaten our self-esteem the first time we learn that we aren't the most beautiful person in the class, or the smartest person on the test, and so forth. And we develop ways to deal with these threats as we grow and mature.

What makes science different in this regard is that doing science requires us to make our beliefs explicit and then test them against reality. For example, suppose that you believe that people who experience frustration will tend to become aggressive. A scientist who wishes to test this idea will devise a situation in which it will be possible to find out if that belief is true or false. In other words, we deliberately set ourselves up so that our idea can be proven wrong. In fact, philosophers say that we should set up our experiments so that we *try* to prove our ideas wrong. According to this notion, we are *successful* when we *fail* to knock our ideas down, not when we find evidence *for* them.

Science is one of the few human activities where we deliberately and systematically set out to prove our beliefs wrong, or at least to put our beliefs at risk. We should not be surprised to find that doing this arouses some anxiety, and that not everyone is prepared to undertake it.

> **Exercise:** Write down some things you have learned in this class that have caused you anxiety because they challenged something you believed. Now do the same thing for some things you learned in everyday life. How are they similar?

Section 8

But the Book Says...

Principle: *Beware of secondary sources.*

Sometime before your psychology course is over, your instructor will probably say, "Your book says such and so, but it is really thus and so." The chances are that your instructor may know something that the authors of the text didn't know. You shouldn't be surprised by this. No one knows everything, and just because it is written in a book doesn't mean it is right.

A journal that publishes an experiment is called a *primary source*, because that is where you go to get the original description of some research. Books that review experiments published in the original sources are called *secondary sources*. Writers of textbooks often rely on secondary sources for their information. Therefore, if the secondary source got it wrong, the textbook will, too.

Here's an example from my own area of expertise. Many introductory psychology books have a figure in the chapter on the senses that shows how sensitivity to salty, sour, sweet, and bitter tastes vary over the surface of the tongue. They show an area at the tip that is sensitive to sweet, two areas a little to either side that are sensitive to salty, two farther back along either side that are sensitive to sour, and a single area in the back of the tongue that is sensitive to bitter.

Only one problem: It isn't so. It is true that sensitivity to the different taste qualities varies *somewhat* over the tongue, and the areas listed are for the most part the ones most sensitive to the various tastes. But with the exception of the middle of the tongue, which is totally insensitive to any taste, *all areas of the tongue are sensitive to all taste qualities.*

Why should you believe me instead of your textbook? I could say that I am an expert in taste and so I know about these things. But better, you can easily demonstrate this for yourself. Lick your finger and dip it in the sugar bowl. Then touch your finger to various parts of your tongue. You will easily taste the sugar on all parts of the tongue except the middle, where you can't taste anything. (You won't be able to touch your finger to the back of the tongue without gagging. You could try reaching that area with a long handled Q-tip.)

Then why does your book have this wrong information? Well, back in 1901 a man named Hanig identified differences in taste sensitivity across the tongue and published his results in the form of a map of the tongue. This map found its way into textbooks and has been copied from one book to another ever since.

Now two things are interesting about Hanig's results. First, he did *not* say that only certain areas were sensitive to the four taste qualities. He said that certain areas were *more* sensitive than others. The textbooks that copied each other dropped this subtlety, something like what happens in the party game Rumor.

The second interesting thing about Hanig's data is that for seventy three years *no one ever replicated his results,* until Virginia Collings did so in my laboratory. As did Hanig, she also found that the differences between areas were small, on the order of 2 or 3 to 1. This difference is quite trivial when one considers that the tongue must respond over a range of at least tens of thousands to 1.

So a result that was found only once was parroted for decades by books, and not even correctly, because they copied from one another instead of going back to look at the original source.

Do you suppose that Collings's experiment corrected the situation? It has been 20 years since she published her data, and various review articles have pointed out the actual situation, but the wrong maps keep showing up in textbooks. I expect to see these wrong maps for a long time to come.

Exercise: Ask your instructor if there is something in your textbook that she or he finds to be incorrect.

Section 9

But I Read It in a Book!

Principle: *Most sources of information available to the general
public are produced by people motivated by profit and
therefore should be considered as entertainment.* Caveat
emptor *(let the buyer beware).*

I encourage my students to bring clippings from the newspaper to
class for discussion. But when they do, I frequently have to say, "Well, I'd
take that with a grain of salt." To which they reply, "But how could it be in
a book (or on television, or in a magazine) if it weren't true?"

Students are often surprised to learn that there is no law against publishing things in a book that aren't true. Now I am not talking about fiction,
which doesn't pretend to be true. I am talking about books that claim that
such-and-such happened when it never did. Some time ago, a book was
published as nonfiction (that is, as fact) that described how a man had been
cloned. There was quite a flap when it turned out that the story was fiction,
because it had been portrayed as fact—but no law had been broken.

To be sure, a person can be sued if he libels someone in a book, or a
professor faces legal problems if she publishes a paper claiming to have
done a certain experiment when she didn't. But there is no law against simply publishing untruths.

This situation is similar to the one we discussed in Section 8, where
we talked about the fact that textbooks aren't always accurate. The difference is that textbooks try to hold to a very high standard of accuracy. They
have to, or professors wouldn't adopt them for their classes. But here we

are talking about books in general, as well as magazines, television, radio, movies—the media.

We could discuss many examples where the media have not been particularly accurate in portraying facts. A few years ago, the movie *JFK* portrayed the assassination of President Kennedy as a giant conspiracy. I recall a conversation with one person who urged me to see it because he found it very thought provoking. My answer was that it contradicted known facts and made other claims for which there was no evidence. Therefore, I saw no reason why watching a work of fiction would help me decide who killed JFK.

Books on ESP and related topics also serve as a good example of what we are talking about. There are many such books, and the vast majority of them claim that ESP exists. Some years ago, I decided that there was a need for a book that told the other side of the story, and so I began to write a manuscript. I wrote several chapters and sent them off to a number of publishers, which is the usual way to get a book published. Each one wrote back and told me that the material was very interesting, but there was no market for such a book. One major publisher, whose name most people would recognize, told me that they would be happy to publish my book if I would just change my conclusion and say that ESP does exist! (Since that time, a publishing company by the name of Prometheus Books has been founded specifically to produce books that are skeptical of the idea of ESP, and they have published a number of such books. But the fact remains that the vast majority of books on ESP are favorable to the notion.)

Why are so few skeptical books published? The simple fact is that the vast majority of books are published by people who want to make a profit. If a particular book is likely to make a profit, it will be published; otherwise it won't. And this is true of all the media. They produce books, programs, and films that people will pay to read or watch. We could go into considerable detail on the misinformation and lack of balance in documentaries on television about the Loch Ness monster, Noah's ark, ESP, or whatever. Just remember that television and books are considered entertainment, and their producers need to make a profit.

I can give another personal example of media bias. A few years ago, when the Israeli "psychic" Uri Geller was at the peak of his popularity, he was scheduled to appear on a talk show on a major Pittsburgh radio station as part of his tour of the United States. It so happened that I was teaching a class on ESP at the time, and I had just discussed Geller and how he did his magic tricks. It also happened that the producer of the show was a student in my class. She invited me to appear on the show the night after Geller to discuss his methods. I agreed, rather reluctantly, because I knew that scientists who take on psychics often get more than they bargain for. (Geller has since sued several people who have criticized him in public.)

But then she called me back and said, sheepishly, that she would have to disinvite me. It turned out that her boss at the station had vetoed my appearance on the show. He told her that they were in the entertainment business, and debunking is not entertaining. So you need to realize that almost every source of information available to the average person is ruled by the profit motive. In other words, the bottom line is the bottom line.

Who, then, can you trust? You probably won't be surprised learn that I think that professors and their writings in scholarly books and journals are more reliable than the commercial media. I am not saying that professors are more noble than other people. I am not saying that they are unbiased. It is just that professors have much more freedom to say what they believe to be true. One time after I appeared on a local radio station debunking ESP, an irate woman called the university and tried to get me fired. She seemed to think that having a skeptic teach ESP was equivalent to having an atheist teach religion. But I have tenure, and the university respects academic freedom, so she was politely told to go fry ice.

Professors are not as affected by market forces as most other writers. They publish their work in journals that don't have to make a profit and in books that are not intended for a mass market. They seek to impress their fellow professors, not people who listen to radio talk shows. So they are much more likely to be reliable than the commercial media. To be sure, a small number of magazines and books intended for the general public are usually reliable, but they are in the minority.

Exercise: Look through a supermarket tabloid newspaper for a story that relates to psychology. List some questions you would ask yourself before you would believe the story.

Section 10

But It Was a Psychology Book!

Principle: *Scientific books and journals document the claims they make.*

This point is similar to that made in Section 9. Not only are some books, such as textbooks, more reliable than others because they are written by people who place a high value on accuracy, but some sources are more reliable because they document their claims.

You may have had the experience of reading about an interesting new scientific finding in the newspaper or a magazine and then deciding that you would like to do more reading about the subject. You may have looked in vain through the article for information that would permit you to find out more. It may have quoted a Professor So-and-So without giving an address. Some articles, on the other hand, particularly in major newspapers and magazines, will say something like, "In the June issue of the *Journal of Experimental Psychology,* Professor So-and-So reports that..." This at least gives you a start.

But often you will read a claim in a book or magazine without any leads for finding out more about the subject. In Section 11 we discuss the book, *Subliminal Seduction,* by Wilson Bryan Key (1973). This book and several like it by Mr. Key claim to present scientific information about how subliminal advertising. mostly of a sexual nature, is manipulating the public. Many of my students have read this book, and found it convincing. It is most instructive, however, to see how Key documents his claims. He presents five pages of references, which seem pretty impressive until you look at them closely.

In a scientific book, you expect to see references to articles that described the original research. Original research is generally published in journals that have an elaborate process of review by other scientists before the articles come out. Secondary sources, such as textbooks, are generally based on the original research and give specific information in a reference list about where you can read more about the work being discussed.

By contrast, the typical references in Key's book are to other general audience books much like his own—if you try to find the source of his quotes, you will end up going in circles. Typical books in Key's reference list are Eric Byrne's *Games People Play*, or Eldridge Cleaver's *Soul on Ice*. The first is pop psych, and the second is a memoir. The few in his list that are themselves scientific do not specifically back up his claims.

As a matter of fact, although the section of the book is labeled "References," what you really have is just a list of books that may or may not have anything to do with what Key says in his book. The books are not necessarily referred to (hence the term *reference*) in the book. They are just listed at the end, with the implication that they support what he is saying, without showing what the connection might be.

By contrast, a scientific book will provide a notation at the place where a particular idea is being discussed so that you can look in the reference list for the specific information you need to track down more about the subject. And further, the index will usually list the place in the book where a certain person's work is discussed. In popular books like Key's, however, the ideas just float there without any way of finding more about them, or finding where they actually come from. If you do look up the books listed at the end of such a book, you generally find you are on a wild goose chase, because the other books either have very little to do with the book you started with, or they are more of the same.

Now I focused on Key's book because it claims to be based on empirical evidence (facts), and my students ask about it frequently. Nevertheless, because this one is getting a little long in the tooth, I will mention a few recent examples that can easily be found on bookstore shelves today.

The Road Less Traveled: A New Psychology of Love, Traditional Values, and Spiritual Growth, the megahit by M. Scott Peck (1978), has only some 24 references, a rather skimpy number given its 315 pages, and a good many of them are to poetry. *The Power Within! Tap Your Inner Force and Program Yourself for Success*, by James K. Van Fleet (1994), has eight references, four of them to other books by Mr. Van Fleet. *Born for Love*, by Leo Buscaglia (1992) (sometimes known as Dr. Love), has no references. *Obsessive Love: When It Hurts Too Much to Let Go*, by Susan Foreward and Craig Buck (1992), has no references, but 10 suggested readings.

I could give many more examples. But Robert Sardello takes the cake, in my experience. He tries to turn the lack of references in his book, *Facing the World with Soul* (1994), into a virtue with the following pompous twaddle:

In Lieu of References

Dear Friend:

Since the purpose of these letters has not been to exhibit a non-existent erudition but always to try and point to the world as teacher, I do not wish to send you off to read the invaluable works that through the years have stimulated and formed my imagination. I will however name some books you may also pass through as itinerant travelers seeking soul. (p. 187)

This announcement is followed by a list of about 50 books and/or authors.

Remember, there is nothing wrong with reading a secondary source. The book you are now reading is, for the most part, a secondary source, because it is mostly based on the original work of others. But secondary sources should give you references to their original sources if they claim to be scientific.

Exercise: Browse the popular psychology section of any bookstore. Examine the back of the books to see how they document their claims. How does it compare to your psychology textbook?

Section 11

But Everybody Knows...

Principle: Many things that "everyone knows" simply aren't true. Ask for the documentation.

For many years students have asked me about the experiment in which the words "Eat Popcorn" and "Drink Coca Cola" flashed subliminally on the screen at a movie dramatically increased sales. And for many years I would shrug my shoulders and say that it was hard for me to comment because I had never seen the details of the experiment written up in a scientific journal.

Eventually, I read a report of the experiment in the popular book *Subliminal Seduction,* by Wilson Bryan Key (1973). Intrigued, I looked in the back of the book for a reference to the article to see where I could read more about it. I found five pages of references, but none that appeared to have any relation to the experiment. (Significantly, as discussed in Section 10, you will look in vain in that book for references to journals where original psychological research is published.)

After that, I began making an offer to my students of a cash reward for the first one who could bring me the reference to the original article on the "Eat Popcorn" study. I made the offer in good faith, because I really wanted to see how it was done. When no one could come up with the reference, I kept increasing the reward, but still no reference.

Eventually, I discovered that *the experiment had never been done.* According to the detective work of Stuart Rogers (1992–1993), the story had been made up out of whole cloth by a man named James M. Vicary, who used it to generate millions of dollars in business for his marketing consult-

29

ing business. When he apparently had gotten enough money to retire on, he disappeared, leaving no bank accounts, no clothes in his closet, and no forwarding address.

This is probably one of the most famous psychology experiments of all time, judging by the fact that almost everyone has heard of it. Yet it never happened!

It is interesting to ask why this imaginary experiment has gotten so thoroughly embedded in our cultural memory. It seems to have many of the qualities of an urban legend, those things that everyone knows that aren't so, such as the alligators that supposedly live in the New York City sewer system. Sociologists tell us that urban legends must be plausible and must appeal to some deep fears that everyone has. In the case of the alligators, it is the fear that one of the critters will rear up out of the toilet when we are sitting on it and bite off our private parts. Castration anxiety (at least for males) in Freud's terms. In the case of subliminal perception, it is the fear that we could be manipulated without our knowledge.

So we should look for documentation for claims that are made.

Exercise: Read any paragraph in your textbook. Notice how claims are documented by references to articles and books listed in the reference list in the back of the book. Do you find any important claims made, or experiments described, that you could not read about in an original source?

Section 12

I Thought Psychology Was about People, Not Numbers!

Principle: Science requires publicly observable, reliable data.

Many students sign up for introductory psychology expecting to learn how to get along with their roommates better, have success with the opposite sex, and so forth. They are frustrated when the instructor jumps into a discussion of research methods, statistics, and other stuff that seems far removed from people. Worse yet, psychology seems to treat people as numbers, not as living, human beings.

This frustration comes from a misunderstanding of what psychology is about. As you have no doubt heard from your instructor, psychology is a science, not just a profession or an art. This statement is made so often in psychology classes that students sometimes wonder if it is some kind of mantra to get us into the proper state to talk about psychology.

Many people's idea of what psychology is comes from guest "experts" who dispense dubious advice on talk shows. You should realize that many people who have slender credentials see fit to use the good name of psychology to improve their status in the eyes of the public. The fact is that the field of psychology is rather different from the popular notion of it, and psychology in actuality involves much more research than most people realize.

Even those who practice psychology, rather than doing research, base their practice on research. This is why virtually everyone who wants to become a psychologist has to study research methods (see Section 5). So psychology spends a good deal of time talking about research—in other words, numbers. The reason is simple: In order to be a scientist, you have to measure things. Measurement is one of the main things that separates science from similar disciplines that are not science.

Measuring people's behavior in the form of numbers forces scientists to be precise about what they are talking about: "Oh, I see. When she says 'spouse abuse,' she means how many times the partner caused an injury requiring medical attention." This is called an *operational definition*. It defines the concept by the operations with which we measure it. The operational definition of spouse abuse just given certainly doesn't include all possible behaviors that might be considered abusive. There may be better definitions, but even this one gives us a way of counting incidents, comparing differences between groups, looking for trends over time, and so on. In brief, numbers increase the precision of our observations.

An operational definition does something else. It makes it possible for anyone else to count the incidents of spouse abuse exactly the same way. This is how the data of science become publicly observable: Anyone who cares to do so can look at the same situation and make the same observation. This is what makes experiments *replicable* (repeatable). In other words, the data are objective. Objectivity here simply means that everyone will agree on how many incidents of spouse abuse there were; it doesn't mean that someone else couldn't have defined the term differently or that the observation was made by a robot.

The advantages that flow from the application of numbers, or *quantification,* are so great that it is often said that the scientific status of a discipline can be gauged by the extent to which it makes use of numbers. Numbers not only improve the precision of our discussion, they permit us to derive and test models with a power that mere words never can. It is one thing to say that the earth goes around the sun in a sort of a loop. But saying that the earth follows an elliptical path permits us to model it mathematically and to predict events like the winter solstice and solar eclipses with great precision.

Although psychology is unlikely to be confused with astronomy on the basis of its mathematical elegance, the mathematical sophistication of its theoretical models is much greater than would be surmised from reading an introductory textbook. A glance at a journal such as *The Psychological Review* will probably surprise most students by the amount of math needed to understand the articles in it.

> **Exercise:** How would defining violent incidents operationally help one to study the amount of violence on different TV programs? How would that reduce that subjectivity involved in comparing different programs?

Section 13

Why Do We Have to Learn about the Brain?

Principle: *A knowledge of the biology of the human organism can provide many insights into its behavior.*

Almost every introductory psychology text has at least one chapter on the brain. Although some students find this among the most interesting topics in the course, others wonder why it is necessary to learn material that appears to belong in a biology text.

As you have probably noticed from the topics covered in your textbook, psychology is a very broad and heterogeneous field. Some areas are far removed from biology, and others seem more biology than psychology. But one of the direct historical roots of psychology is physiology, the branch of biology that studies the function of various organ systems. And there has been a close connection between psychology and biology ever since.

Considering psychology as a biological science has a number of advantages. First, it permits us to see human behavior as having a great deal in common with that of other animals. From this perspective, we are not surprised to see that animal research can tell us a great deal about our own thought processes. This is the main reason so many psychologists have spent their careers studying learning in rats, perception in pigeons, problem solving in apes, and the like.

Second, a biological perspective suggests that we should be able to see how evolutionary processes have shaped our behavior. Psychologists have recently used the theory of evolution to help understand such human phenomena as dating preferences, spousal abuse, and gender differences in spatial perception.

Third, some remarkable insights into psychological processes have come from witnessing the effects of interfering with the biology of the organism. Some of the most striking discoveries come from cases of individuals who have suffered strokes, or other brain damage. The change in behavior seen in these unfortunate persons makes it abundantly clear that a knowledge of how the brain works can help understand human behavior.

Take the classic case of Phineas Gage, who in 1848 was the foreman of a work crew building a new line for the Rutland and Burlington Railroad in Vermont (Macmillan, 1986). Gage was tamping gunpowder in a hole in order to blast some rock when a spark ignited the powder, causing a terrible explosion. The rod, which was 3.5 feet long and an 1.25 inches thick, blasted into his skull beneath his eye, went out the top of his head, and landed about 50 yards away.

Phineas Gage not only survived the explosion, he barely lost consciousness and eventually recovered, after a fashion. But his behavior was forever changed. Previously a sociable, responsible person, he became profane, had an evil temper, and could not hold down a regular job. He wound up making a living as a fairground attraction.

Phineas Gage provided one of the earliest and most dramatic demonstrations of the fact that various psychological functions are localized in different parts of the brain, contrary to the view popular at the time that the brain worked as a unit, something like a muscle for thinking. We now know that the frontal lobes, which were destroyed in Phineas Gage's case, are responsible for planning and carrying out complex activities—precisely what Gage was unable to do after his accident.

Since the time of Phineas Gage, we have learned a great deal about the sorts of changes that can be produced by brain damage. Some stroke victims, for example, are unable to recognize faces, even though they can see and recognize other objects. They may even be able to describe other features associated with the face—mustache, hat, cigar, and so on. We have also learned a great deal about which parts of the brain are involved in these functions. So it should be no surprise that psychologists are interested in how the brain works.

Exercise: Look in the chapter in your textbook on the brain for a psychological finding that could not be understood without a knowledge of how the brain works.

Section 14

But Can We Really Understand Behavior until We Know Its Biological Basis?

Principle: *Many psychological processes are emergent properties of organisms and cannot be reduced to a more basic level of analysis.*

This question is, of course, the flip side of the last one, which asked why we need to know how the brain works. The question assumes that in order to understand a behavioral phenomenon we need to explain it at a more basic level than behavior—namely biology.

The idea that we understand a process by explaining it at a more basic level of analysis is called *reductionism.* Thus, some people would say that we really understand a psychological process such as learning by explaining it in terms of biochemical processes, such as changes in neurotransmitters in the brain. We would understand the biochemistry of neurotransmitters in turn by explaining it in terms of physics, and so forth. (The "so forth" is one of the problems with this notion, because where do you stop?)

Another problem with reductionism is that not everything can be reduced to a more basic level. Some properties are *emergent*—that is, they appear unpredictably at a given level of complexity and can't be reduced to a lower level because they do not exist at that level. In the course of evolution, for example, organs such as the brain developed whose functions could not be explained in terms of the neurons of which they were composed. Nor could you have predicted how brains would work based on the behavior of individual neurons until they appeared in the course of evolution.

Perhaps the clearest example of an emergent property is the behavior of a computer. Computers are made out of electronic components that obey all the laws of electronics. But programming a computer has everything to do with mathematics and logic, and nothing to do with electronics. In order to understand the behavior of computers, it is necessary to understand how they are programmed. A program can be entered into computers with very different electronics and it will behave exactly the same in each one. In fact, it's theoretically possible to build a computer out of Tinkertoys. So it would be impossible to understand how a computer works by reducing the program to electronics. The program must be understood as a logical system at its own level.

Many (but not all) psychological processes are also emergent, in that they cannot be predicted from simpler processes on which they are built. Some psychological processes that may qualify as emergent are consciousness, group coalition formation, and operant conditioning.

Let's consider operant conditioning as an example. Concepts used in understanding conditioning include *reinforcer, discriminative stimulus,* and *schedule of reinforcement.* None of these terms can be explained in terms of the structure or function of the brain. They are emergent properties that cannot be reduced to a more basic level.

So although understanding the biological basis of behavior is important, as we argued in the previous unit, it is a mistake to insist that we *only* understand a phenomenon by reducing it to a more basic level of analysis.

Exercise: Which of the following explanations are reductionistic, and which are not?

1. Brad's depression was caused by a chemical imbalance in the brain.
2. Brad's depression was caused by his thinking that his problems were beyond his control.
3. After Mr. H. suffered a stroke in the left frontal lobe of his brain, he was unable to speak.
4. Jeff kicked the soda pop machine when it didn't have his favorite brand, illustrating the frustration-aggression law.

(Answers: 1 and 3)

Section 15

How Does the Mind Control the Body?

Principle: *Most psychologists are monists. That is, they believe that mind is another word for the workings of the brain.*

René Descartes was a French philosopher around the turn of the seventeenth century. Descartes wondered how the mind controlled the body. He thought of the mind as a nonphysical entity that somehow interacted with the physical body. He chose the pineal body of the brain as the seat of the mind for two reasons: First, it was the only part of the brain he knew of that was single—every other structure seemed to come in pairs, and the mind was obviously (to him) unitary. Second, the pineal body lies close to the ventricles, which he thought had mental functions.

Descartes was wrong in both of his reasons for choosing the pineal body as the seat of the mind. First, the pituitary body is also not a paired structure, but he didn't know that. Second, the ventricles have no direct mental function.

But most psychologists, neuroscientists, and others who study with the brain believe that Descartes was wrong in a different, and more fundamental, way. They do not believe that the mind is a different sort of stuff from the brain—"mental," "spiritual," or whatever. They believe that the term *mind* is a kind of shorthand, or informal, way of referring to the working of the brain. In other words, the mind is what the brain does.

This modern position is known as *materialistic monism.* It is monistic because it holds that there is only one kind of reality, or "stuff." It is materialistic because it holds that the one kind of stuff is material, not mental, or spiritual. To be sure, other possibilities exist.

One alternative is to suppose that there is a physical world and a mental world. This position is called *dualism*. Descartes' brand of dualism is called *interactive dualism* because he thought the mind could influence the brain. Dualists, however, have the problem of explaining how a nonmaterial mind can interact with a material brain. Descartes thought he knew *where* the interaction took place, but scientists today do not think he explained *how* it worked.

Interestingly enough, although we believe Descartes was wrong in his view of the interaction between the mind and the body, he actually had made a great step forward. He believed that a great deal of what we call mental processes, including *all* of an animal's behavior, could be accounted for by understanding the brain alone. He invoked the mind only for the purely human processes underlying consciousness, free choice, and rationality, which he denied to animals (Hergenhahn, 1992).

Finally, we should mention that some psychologists would agree to consider the mind as the workings of the brain *for the purpose of doing science*, without necessarily agreeing that this is the way things *really are*. In other words, they may make a *methodological* assumption of monism when they do science, because that seems to be the way science must work. But in their heart of hearts they may believe that there is more than a material world.

> **Exercise:** Consider that nonhuman apes are capable of many higher cognitive processes, including communication by means of computers. Where does that leave Descartes' need for a nonmaterial mind? What if it could be shown that an ape is conscious, has free will, and can think rationally?

Section 16

But Why Don't We Talk about What the Mind Really Is?

Principle: To try to study what something really is is to commit the philosophical error of essentialism.

This is one of the most common objections to psychology as it is practiced by researchers and taught in college courses. Many students take psychology expecting to learn about the mind and are disappointed at best—or worse, alienated—when they find that they have only learned some things about perception, learning, memory, and so on instead. They sometimes complain that we don't talk about what the mind really is; we study how it works and ignore its essence—its basic nature, or ultimate reality.

This is one complaint about psychology that is perfectly accurate: Psychologists in fact don't worry much about what the mind really is. They spend their time studying how it works. We leave the problem of what the mind is to the philosophers. It is true that psychologists have some opinions of what the mind is: Most psychologists believe that the mind is what the brain does. In other words, they consider the mind to be the activity of the brain, which is, of course, an organ of the body.

Although the complaint is accurate, it reflects a misunderstanding of what scientists do. Biologists study life, but you will wait a very long time before you hear a biologist trying to define what life is. I remember as a freshman biology student learning that several processes were characteristic of living things: growth, metabolism, reproduction, and so on. But these processes do not define life, they are simply some important properties that living things display. You can study biology for as long as you want and not be any closer to the essence of life.

If you object that psychologists fail to capture the essence of the human mind, you are both right and wrong at the same time. You are right because scientists never capture the essence of anything. You are wrong because you should not expect science to tell you the essence of the human mind or of anything else. That is outside the purview of science.

Perception, learning, memory, and so forth are all *processes*: *how* we perceive, *how* we learn, *how* we remember. We theorize about how the mind *works*, not what it *is*. Failure to make this distinction between a thing and the function of that thing is sometimes called the error of *essentialism*.

For another example, we use the terms *beauty* and *beautiful* to refer to many things and many actions: flowers, music, kind words. It would be fruitless to try to discover what is common to all of these uses of the word *beauty*. There is no essence of beauty, abstract concept of beauty, or ideal form of beauty in the sky somewhere.

Essentialism is a problem in many parts of psychology, but particularly when we talk about consciousness. For one thing, the term *consciousness* (together with its adjectival form, *conscious*) has many different meanings. We say that someone is conscious as opposed to asleep, that someone is conscious of where she is, that a fact is available to consciousness, and so on. Each of these uses is different and can usually be understood by the context.

To assume that one thing is common to all these uses of the term *consciousness* is to make the mistake of thinking that just because we use the same word each time there has to be some essential meaning common to all uses, when in fact it has many meanings depending on how we use it.

Many psychologists who study cognition will speak of a thought existing "in consciousness," as when we are aware at a given moment of a person's name. They may also talk about the role of consciousness in thought, as when we consciously work on an arithmetic problem. From this usage, some people assume that consciousness is a thing or a place. They sometimes go further and try to theorize about what kind of a thing consciousness is.

The fact is, consciousness isn't anything. That is, it isn't any *thing*. Consciousness is a property of some mental processes, and not of others. If we worry about what consciousness is, we are getting sidetracked by the fallacy of essentialism.

The uselessness of trying to define consciousness is seen by examining the question of whether a computer can ever be conscious. Some people find this an intriguing question. The argument goes that as computers become more and more complicated and have more of the properties of the human brain, they will eventually become conscious, because we are conscious. The reason this line of speculation is useless is because we can't even define consciousness in the case of ourselves. How can we then define it for another sort of entity?

What is fruitful is to ask specific questions about the role of consciousness, as defined by a particular situation. For example, psychologists study whether learning a particular task is better if subjects consciously think about the rule that governs the task. In such an experiment, subjects may be asked to state out loud their guesses about the solution of a puzzle as they work on it. The question is whether they will learn faster than subjects who just work at the puzzle. Here consciousness is defined as stating guesses out loud. That is all.

The error of essentialism pops up in many places. We mentioned earlier the impossibility of defining life. It follows that defining death will be equally impossible. When people begin to worry about how to define death for the purpose of removing organs for transplantation, the biologists are not much help. It is the ethicists and lawyers who are called in to help decide when a person should be declared dead. The biologist can tell when the heart has stopped beating, or respiration has ceased, or the brain waves are flat. But doctors and family members need to make a very different, and intensely ethical, decision that someone is dead for the purpose of permitting a heart transplant.

Similarly, biologists are no help in defining when life begins for the purpose of deciding whether abortion should be legal. True, the fetus is human tissue. What else could it be? But so is the placenta, sperm, blood, and other tissues that are not accorded the same treatment as a person. At some point the fertilized egg grows into a person with human status and rights, but biology will be of little, if any, help in deciding when that line is crossed.

Exercise: Think of another example where trying to define the essence of something leads to confusion.

Section 17

But People Aren't Machines!

Principle: *Science looks for mechanisms to explain behavior.*

The fact is, people *are* machines: Our muscles and bones constitute a mechanical lever system; our heart is a pump; and our eye is like a camera. Further, it is a basic task of science to take some human function and try to discover a mechanism that will model it.

When psychologists started to study how we perceive the world, they learned that an image of the world is projected onto the retina of the eye much as a camera projects an image of the world on the film inside it. The problem was, how is the image then interpreted by the brain? In the absence of a mechanistic explanation of perception, psychologists of the day proposed that there must be something in the head that interpreted the image. This something was called the *homunculus,* which literally means little man. The homunculus was supposed to look at the image and turn it into a perception. The problem was—and it was a very big problem—how did the homunculus work? In other words, to say that the homunculus did something was no explanation at all; it merely passed the problem one more step along without explaining it at all.

Today we know how certain neurons in the brain respond to particular features of an image of an object that is projected onto the retina. This detailed knowledge has done away with the need for the homunculus because we can describe a mechanism that performs part of the perceptual process. So we have taken the homunculus and replaced it with a neural mechanism. The more we know about perception, the more we can describe processes by which they are carried out. In short, we have replaced the mind with a mechanism.

The purpose of a mechanism is to make a detailed explanation of how a process works. This explanation will consist of elements whose function is already known. When we explain perception in terms of the operation of neurons in the brain, we are replacing an imaginary, nonmechanistic homunculus whose function we don't understand with a real, mechanistic process whose properties are understood. Whereas we had to say that the homunculus *interprets* the image, we can now say that the neurons in the brain *respond* when they receive an input from the eye. The homunculus "explanation" required the little person to be intelligent, so it was no explanation at all. The explanation invoking the neurons makes use of knowledge of how neurons are connected to other neurons (which we have not gone into here). The latter is an explanation because it appeals to something we understand.

You should not conclude from this discussion that all scientific explanations have to be expressed in terms of biological processes, as in the perception example, or in terms of things we can point to. Psychological mechanisms can include the principle that says that frustration causes aggression. It is not necessary to find a part of the brain that is labeled frustration or aggression (see Section 14).

The computer has been a very popular mechanistic model of the human mind in recent years. We are used to computers that act in a manner that can appear very intelligent. They can solve problems, remember, answer questions, and even understand simple speech commands. In brief, they can do many things that people do, usually faster, and often better. When a computer does something that appears intelligent, we have no problem believing that it is done by some mechanism, because we know that a computer is a machine designed by humans. Although we don't automatically assume that the computer is doing humanlike activities in the same way that a human does, we gain some confidence that it is possible for human thought processes to be explained mechanistically. Many cognitive scientists use what is known about the computer to suggest and test mechanisms by which the mind could operate.

Exercise: Think of some psychological process that can be explained by a mechanism.

Section 18

Is It True That We Use Only 10% of Our Brains?

Principle: *Sometimes we hold beliefs simply because they have useful implications, not because of any evidence.*

This supposed fact is one of the hardiest weeds in the garden of psychology. Probably everyone has been exhorted by a teacher to work harder because "we only use 10% of our brains—imagine what we could do if we used 100%."

Let's get it straight—this isn't true. It is one of those things that "everyone knows" that just isn't so. In fact, how could it possibly be so? Stop and think about it: What could this statement possibly mean? That we could do without 90% of our brain? Ask the next person who tells you this "fact" which part of the brain he or she would like to have removed.

Or does it mean that we could all be Einsteins if we tried? Most of us could do somewhat better in school—but 10 times better?

Or does it mean that we could work 10 times harder? May be a few could do 10 times more than they do, but all of us? We would burn ourselves out pretty quickly if we tried.

Or maybe it means that we could learn music if we tried, or basketball, or painting, or rock climbing, or poetry. Sure, we all have talents we haven't developed. But does that mean there is a part of the brain waiting to do sculpture that we aren't using? It takes only a little knowledge of the brain to realize that most things we do involve large parts of the brain, so there are no chunks of brain tissue sitting around doing nothing.

This belief is but one of many that we hold because it has some usefulness to us, not because it is true. It suggests we should all try to be the best we can—an idea that is hard to disagree with. But we should be careful not to accept a belief just because holding it has some benefit. If we did, we would all believe we were the most intelligent, charming, handsome/beautiful person on the planet, because it would make us feel terrific. The only problem is that we are probably not. (The chances are one in 5 billion that we are.)

But we all have a tendency to believe things that we like to believe. We believe that our mothers love us, that the U.S. government will not go broke, that the sky will not fall. All of these things are true—we hope—and we don't waste much time worrying about them. But we tend to believe some other things to be true that may not be: that we can control our future, that if we eat well and exercise we will live to a ripe old age, and so on.

One antidote to our tendency to believe things we like to believe is to ask ourselves what the consequences would be if the belief were true: If I were the most charming person in the world, would I be sitting here reading this book on a Friday night instead of being the guest of honor at a White House dinner?

Unfortunately, questioning beliefs can make us very uncomfortable (see Section 7). What if our mother doesn't really love us? So people tend not to practice this sort of critical thinking. But exercising this skill is an important part of everyday common sense, particularly when someone is trying to convince us to part with some money, or our belief systems: Say, Mable, how can royal jelly from queen bees be good for your skin when bees don't even have skin?

> **Exercise:** Following are two statements you may have heard that illustrate beliefs that may be useful even if not true. Think of three more.
>
> 1. You can achieve whatever you set your mind to do.
> 2. Every day, in every way, I am getting better and better.

Section 19

Why Don't Psychologists Believe in Punishment?

Principle: *Regression to the mean is a very common problem in interpreting behavior.*

There are several reasons most psychologists don't believe in punishment: Behavior that is punished is only suppressed temporarily, not forgotten. Further, punishment doesn't teach what behavior will be rewarded. Perhaps most significantly, it has undesirable side effects, such as causing aggressiveness, resentment, and depression (cf. Myers, 1995).

Millions of parents, however, firmly believe that punishment is effective, and many of those who have studied any psychology think psychologists are just plain nuts when it comes to punishment. To them it is obvious that punishment works; moreover, a few even think that reward doesn't work.

As a matter of fact, there are situations in which punishment seems to work and reward doesn't. Consider the case of a parent who has been watching the kids all day and has noticed that they have been exceptionally well-behaved. As a special treat for their good behavior, she decides to take them all out to McDonald's and then go to the store to let them pick out a video. But when they get to McDonald's, one cries because he can't have two Big Macs and the other races around the store, annoying the other customers. The situation at the video store is even worse. They fight over which video to rent, and one throws a tantrum. At her wit's end, she threatens not to take them to McDonald's for a month and decides that rewarding behavior is no use.

A second parent has been watching the kids all day, and they have been nothing but a pain in the neck. It seems that they have done one thing after another just to annoy him; finally, out of desperation, he turns off the TV and sends them all to their rooms. After a screaming fuss, they finally settle down and come out of their rooms like little angels. He decides that they were just asking to be punished and were really happier after he showed them who was in charge.

Let's assume that this sort of scenario plays out a number of times. These parents compare notes and conclude that rewarding good behavior does no good, but punishment works. Let's also assume that the parents are right in their observation of their kids' behavior. When they reward them for being especially good, they generally get worse, and when they punish them for being particularly bad, they usually get better.

The problem is, even though the parents' observations are correct, their explanation is wrong. They are falling prey to a statistical phenomenon called *regression to the mean*. Consider that when the kids were exceptionally well-behaved, there was no possibility of improvement—they could only get worse. Conversely, when they were acting like little monsters, there was nowhere to go but up. So they were bound to get worse after reward and better after punishment, even if neither one had any effect at all.

Regression to the mean is a very common problem in interpreting behavior. It may occur whenever two behaviors are correlated or when the same behavior is measured twice. Unless the two measures are perfectly correlated, the second one will, *one the average,* be less extreme than the first. The reason has to do with random error that enters into the measurement. If the kids' behavior varied from day to day on a random basis, then it would be just luck whether they were good or bad. And it would take a lot of luck for them to be especially good (or bad). So it is not likely that the luck will hold the second time you measure their behavior. Thus, especially good or bad behavior won't continue.

A good example of regression to the mean is given by the so-called *Sports Illustrated* jinx. That magazine puts outstanding athletes on its cover. It is widely believed that this exposure jinxes the players because their performance so often takes a nosedive afterwards. But consider that getting onto the cover of *Sports Illustrated* requires not only that you be very talented, but that a lot of other things have to go just right—in other words you need a lot of luck. It stands to reason that luck tends to run out, and the performance has nowhere to go but down.

In an experiment, Paul Schaffner (1985) presented his subjects with computerized descriptions of the promptness or tardiness of an imaginary schoolboy over a large number of trials. He asked his subjects to reward or punish the schoolboy appropriately after each trial as they saw fit.

Afterwards, the subjects believed that the punishments they had administered had been effective but the rewards had been ineffective.

In fact, the promptness of the imaginary schoolboy had been completely random, and his behavior had absolutely nothing to do with the rewards and punishments. But the subjects had correctly noticed that the performance did tend to deteriorate after reward and improve after punishment. Thus, they were not completely wrong in their beliefs. They were just wrong in thinking that they had anything to do with the schoolboy's behavior. This is a clear, experimental parallel to the example of the kids discussed earlier.

Finally, I don't want to leave the impression that regression to the mean only happens when there is no cause-effect relationship between two variables. Reward and punishment do have their effects. But regression to the mean can be so great that it obscures their effects and leads us to the wrong conclusion.

> **Exercise:** Show how each of the following could be an example of regression to the mean.

> 1. Jennifer generally weighs between 120 and 125 pounds, but the weight fluctuates for unknown reasons. Whenever her weight exceeds 125 pounds, she goes on her grapefruit diet and her weight generally returns to the normal range. What else besides the grapefruit diet could be causing her weight to drop?

> 2. Professor Galton notices that students who do especially well on the first test generally drop a few points on the second one, whereas students who do the poorest generally improve next time. He concludes that those who do the best slack off and the ones who do the worst buckle down. What else could be causing this pattern of results?

Section 20

Isn't Psychology Mostly Common Sense?

Principle: *Common sense changes from time to time and is shaped by psychological research, among other influences.*

My father tried to talk me out of going into psychology. "Psychology," he said, "is half common sense—and the other half is nonsense." Now my father was no dummy; he had a master's degree from an Ivy League university. And he had sat through enough psychology courses that his opinion should have carried some weight. (Obviously, I didn't listen to him.) Nor was he alone in his opinion, because I have heard the same thing from other people.

Well, isn't psychology mostly common sense? (We will leave the nonsense part to Section 44.) Certainly, *some* of psychology had better be common sense, because all of us who study psychology in college have already had years of experience in trying to understand why people act the way they do, including ourselves. It would be rather amazing if we didn't have at least a few pretty good ideas about human behavior.

But common sense has severe limitations when it comes to understanding human behavior. First of all, a good deal of human behavior hardly makes sense at all. The mind boggles when we try to imagine the psychology of mass murderer Ted Bundy or humanitarian Mother Teresa, to take two very different cases. And common sense doesn't help us much in dealing with many situations of daily living, let alone understanding how memory, perception, and other processes work.

But the limitation of common sense is revealed by the differences between people in those things that appear as obvious examples of it. Years ago, when people were accused of a crime, their guilt or innocence was test-ed by having them try to chew dry grain and swallow it. A person who could perform this act was considered innocent; one who couldn't was judged guilty. There is a grain of truth in this practice: A person who is guilty is likely to be scared spitless. But innocent persons could well be frightened enough that they couldn't do it, either. Today we have more sci-entific methods of deciding innocence and guilt.

Thus, what appears to be common sense at one time and place may be nonsense in another environment. It wasn't so long ago that most parents believed that the commonsense way to deal with a child who threw a tantrum in a grocery store was to spank him or her—either then and there, or outside the store if they wished to avoid a scene (see Section 19). Nowadays, a child who acts up in public is more likely to receive a *time out*—be placed in an out-of-the-way corner until he or she settles down. And surprising as it still seems to this grandfather, timeouts work remark-ably well. Not incidentally, the practice of giving timeouts is a direct result of psychological research and theory. Further, this is one result of psycho-logical research that has improved the quality of life for millions of chil-dren, their parents, and everyone else within earshot.

So common sense varies from time to time and person to person. And psychology has had a considerable role in shaping what now appears to be common sense. I can see the change in my own attitude toward spanking children since the 1960s, when our children were little. I am often surprised by how distressed I feel now when I witness a child being spanked in pub-lic. (I should say that, although my wife and I did resort to spanking when our children were small, we did so infrequently. As a psychologist, I was aware at the time that it was problematic, although timeouts had not yet come into widespread use.)

> **Exercise:** Talk to a grandparent about how childrearing practices have changed in his or her lifetime. Ask what he or she think of the changes.

Section 21

I Knew It All Along!

Principle: *Events seem more inevitable, likely, or predictable after they occur than they do before. This effect tends to make psychological results less impressive than they otherwise would be.*

The point of this section is somewhat like that of the last one (Section 20), where we talked about the relationship of common sense to psychology. Students sometimes complain that psychology courses tell them what they already know.

Suppose that you are in class and the instructor passes out a slip of paper to each student. You read, "Psychologists have found that couples who have different personalities stay together longer. As the adage says, 'Opposites attract.'" The instructor asks how many people found this result unsurprising. Almost the entire class raise their hands, indicating that they knew it all along.

Then the instructor asks someone else to read her slip of paper, and you hear, "Psychologists have found that couples who have similar personalities stay together longer. As the adage says, 'Birds of a feather flock together'" (Myers, 1992, p. 21). What happened was that half the class read exactly the opposite supposed result as the other half. Nevertheless the vast majority of the class thought the result was obvious, whichever one they read.

This phenomenon is called the I-knew-it-all-along effect, or *hindsight bias.* After the fact, we tend to consider some event or fact to be more obvious than it was before. This impression extends to the results of great battles, presidential elections, and sports events as well as psychological research. It is amusing to read the sports pages the day before and after a big game. The day before, there are all sorts of predictions of the likely outcome. After the game, the commentators confidently explain why it was inevitable that the winner came out on top.

The importance of hindsight bias for psychology is that it tends to make the results of research seem obvious or trivial, even though few could have predicted the results in advance.

> **Exercise:** Take a psychological research finding discussed in your textbook. State the results in a simple sentence, and then in another that says the exact opposite. Give the two versions to a group of people and see how many are surprised by the results. Be sure to tell them the actual facts afterward. (In the example we used earlier, research supports the "birds of a feather" proverb.)

Section 22

Is Human Behavior Based on Nature or Nurture?

Principle: All behavior is influenced by both nature and nurture. It is impossible to say which is more important.

The nature-nurture debate has a long history in psychology, going back to Francis Galton in 1874 (Hergenhahn, 1992). I predict that psychologists 100 years from now will still be arguing about whether heredity or experience is more important. One case in point has to do with the importance of heredity in determining intelligence. Many theorists have argued that intelligence is largely hereditary; others have emphasized environment.

A little reflection reveals that the question has important political implications. If intelligence is mostly hereditary, then differences between groups and classes are part of the natural order and can't be changed very much. If, on the other hand, intelligence is mostly environmental, then public education and social interventions can improve the lot of the underprivileged.

It is apparent to most people that both heredity and environment have some effect on behavior. Thus, at a superficial level we can say that the two interact in producing behavior. A bad environment can keep even the most favorable heredity from showing through, and so forth. But the question gets fairly complicated once we go beyond the obvious truism.

The essential point is that every individual has both a heredity and an environment. It is absolutely impossible to remove the environment and see what the behavior would be. Even the conditions in the womb that nourished the fetus are part of a person's environment. Similarly, every living being has a particular genetic makeup without which it could not exist. So there is no separating the two. It is possible to say in this sense that behavior depends 100% on heredity and 100% on environment.

The only thing we can do is to study *differences* in heredity or in environment and see what *differences* they make in behavior. A technical term that is often used to describe the importance of heredity on behavior, is *heritability*. The heritability of a particular trait is the proportion of the total variability in that trait that can be shown to be caused by heredity. The heritability coefficient varies between 0.0 and 1.0.

The problem comes in interpreting the heritability coefficient. It is tempting to say that zero heritability means the trait is completely dependent on the environment, and 1.0 means it is completely dependent on heredity. But from our earlier discussion we can see that this would be wrong. A heritability coefficient of zero simply means that the *differences* between individuals on a certain trait *in a given population* cannot be accounted for by heredity.

Consider the trait of fearfulness of humans in puppies. Puppies of different breeds of dogs vary in the degree of fear they show toward humans. Some breeds approach humans readily, and others are fearful. Studies in which dogs are cross bred demonstrate that the trait has a high heritability (Scott & Fuller, 1974). Thus, one might conclude that fearfulness in puppies is based on genetics—nature.

But the story changes radically when one realizes that all puppies, regardless of breed, become fearful unless they are handled by humans from birth. If one did an experiment in which various breeds of puppies are either handled or not handled from birth, one would find that most of the variability between dogs would depend on the handling—nurture.

Thus, we see that the degree of heritability depends greatly on the particular environment in which it is measured. So heritability is not a number that permits us to say that so much of behavior is heredity and so much is environment.

Exercise: Consider two hypothetical countries: Country A is a rich country whose children all go to good public schools. Country B is a poor country in which the public schools are inadequate. The wealthy minority sends their children to good private schools. Show how a psychologist might find that heritability of IQ was low in country A and high in country B.

Section 23

Can You Prove There Is No ESP?

Principle: The burden of proof for a claim is on those who make it.

I have had a skeptical interest in ESP for many years, and the word is out around my university that I am the one to talk to about the subject. People frequently say to me, "Can you prove that there is no ESP?"

I always reply along the following lines: "It isn't up to me to prove that there is no such thing as ESP; it is up to those who believe in it to convince me that there is."

Suppose I tell you that I can high-jump 9 feet. If you doubt it (and you should, because the world record is 8 feet, .5 inches, and I don't even look particularly athletic), your obvious response would be: "Show me."

You wouldn't waste any time trying to prove that I couldn't; you wouldn't need to argue that no one in the world has ever done it; you wouldn't have to prove that it would be physically impossible for a human to do it. Instead, you would just ask me to prove it. Put up or shut up.

Suppose I foolishly decided to prove there was no such thing as ESP by doing experiments. Even if I did a million experiments that found no evidence for ESP, that wouldn't prove the phenomenon didn't exist, because the next experiment might prove that it did. A philosopher would say that it is impossible to prove a universal negative. You couldn't prove that there is no Santa Claus and I can't prove that there is no ESP—but I don't have to. Someone has to prove that it does exist.

Most psychologists won't bother with trying to disprove ESP. They will wait until there is good evidence that it does exist. (For a discussion of what would constitute good evidence, see Section 24.)

Exercise: List some mistaken ideas that scientists don't bother disproving.

Section 24

What Would It Take to Make You Believe in ESP?

Principle: *Scientists are convinced of the existence of a phenomenon only when it can be repeated.*

Knowing that I have a skeptical interest in ESP, people often say something like the following to me: "But if you would just do the right experiments, then maybe you could prove that it exists." The fact is, people have done the right experiments for well over 100 years—thousands and thousands of them—and the vast majority of experiments haven't provided any evidence that it exists.

There have been some tantalizing results, and every now and then someone will argue that they are on the verge of proving it once and for all. But the long and the short of it is that there has not been enough of the kind of evidence necessary to convince scientists that it exists.

It is sometimes objected that scientists have closed minds, and are biased against ESP. The answer is simple: Scientists change their minds all the time, when there is sufficient evidence to convince them. Scientists once refused to believed that "stones fall from the sky." A distinguished panel commissioned by the French government even convinced museums to discard precious collections of what we now know to be meteorites. The number of things on which scientists have changed their minds is staggering. (See the discussion of hypnosis, in Section 28.) No, scientists do not have closed minds. They just want proof.

The proof needed in the case of ESP, as in any other area of science, would be repeatable experiments. Scientists sit up and take notice when a repeatable finding shows up. They lose interest when a finding can't be repeated. The results that seem to indicate that ESP exists happen so rarely, and fail the test of replication so often, that scientists discount them as flukes. The recent cold fusion fiasco is an excellent example of how this process works. A few years ago, a pair of scientists claimed that they had managed to produce atomic fusion at room temperature. Up until then (and even now, as it turns out) atomic fusion had required special conditions. If true, cold fusion would have made electricity truly too cheap to meter. A large number of researchers all around the world tried to replicate the results without success, and cold fusion became a footnote in the history of science.

Even researchers who believe in ESP as much as say that the evidence is not convincing. Over and over, articles on ESP start out in their introductions saying something like the following:

> Our goal is to...uncover patterns of cause-effect relationships...in the form with which we are familiar in scientific study. The results presented here constitute a first step toward that goal...a data base [for future work]. (Puthoff & Targ, 1974, p. 602)

Reading between the lines, you can tell that there couldn't have been convincing evidence of ESP when the authors wrote this article, or they wouldn't have been trying to establish a "first step toward a data base." They would have been studying how the phenomenon works.

A recent article in the prestigious *Psychological Bulletin* (Bem & Honorton, 1994) reviews evidence for ESP collected by a certain technique and states:

> We believe that the replication rates and effect sizes are now sufficient to warrant bringing the body of data to the attention of the wider psychological community. (p. 5)

Note that they do not claim to have proven the existence of ESP—just that they think the evidence warrants the attention of psychologists. Note also that they cite the replication rate as a significant factor in their belief in the value of the data. (So far, the wider psychological community appears not to be impressed.)

These quotes are just two examples of many that could be given. But they were chosen because they represent the high water marks over the last quarter century in terms of the prestige of the journals in which articles about ESP have appeared.

Not incidentally, the first article quoted was eventually thoroughly discredited. Time will tell for the second one.

Exercise: Look in your textbook for a discussion of memory transfer by inject-ing DNA from trained rats into naive ones. This was a hot topic about 1960, but it failed to be replicated. Does it appear in the index? If you have a text-book from the 1960s available in your library, compare it to the one you are studying for coverage of that topic.

Section 25

Imagine the Possibilities if ESP Were True!

Principle: One way to evaluate an idea is to try to think of what would happen if it were true—to explore the implications of a theory.

Okay, let's suppose that ESP did exist. How would our world be different? People would be able read each other's minds; they would be able tell the future; they could find lost diamond rings; they could heal the sick without drugs or surgery.

Our world would be very different from what it is if ESP were a fact. Just imagining the possibilities should lead us to be skeptical that it exists. Let's take one example. Many states today have lotteries, and millions of people play them every day. Each person would like to win the jackpot. Some want to retire to Florida; some want to pay off their debts; some want a big car; and so forth. With all these people hoping to win, wouldn't you suppose that this would be a perfect place to test for the existence of ESP?

The fact is that the lotteries behave just the way the laws of chance predict, day in and day out, year after year. Surely if ESP existed, there would be some significant deviation from chance. The simplest prediction would be that too many people would win. They don't. (It isn't necessary that everyone have ESP for the odds not to work—even if only some people had it, the lottery would show distorted results.)

For example, Dale Christopher and I recently analyzed every drawing of the three-digit Pennsylvania Daily Number between March 1, 1977 (the first day ever), and June 2, 1994 (the last day available at the time of this writing) as published in the *Pittsburgh Post Gazette*. To make a long story short, of the ten digits (0–9), the one that deviated most from the frequency expected by chance did so by only 5%. Analyzing all the digits together by a standard statistical methodology showed that the lottery numbers turned up well within the range expected by chance, and far from what statisticians would consider a significant deviation. Many other tests of randomness could be made on these numbers, but they would all show similar results. (Actually, this discussion assumes that people can influence the outcome of the lottery, which would technically be called PK, *psychokinesis*, but I have used the term ESP as a kind of shorthand for a number of alleged paranormal phenomena.)

You might object that you can't use ESP for personal advantage. I have seen this argument made without any apparent reason to back it up. (On the other hand, I know of at least one case where believers in ESP set up a company to give people psychic advice on their investments. After a brief period of apparent success, their luck ran out, as luck always does.)

One might propose any number of ad hoc reasons why you wouldn't see evidence of ESP in the lottery: It has been claimed that ESP is too unpredictable to use for such a purpose, for example. You might say that different people would be pulling for different numbers. (Actually people tend to play certain numbers, such as birth dates, more than others.) But the fact remains that if there were any such thing as ESP, it would *have to* show up as some departure from the laws of chance—say, too *few* people winning, if you can't use it for your own ends. But since ESP is defined *solely* as a deviation from chance, if there are no deviations from chance in the results of the lottery, it makes the existence of such a phenomenon highly unlikely.

We could think of many other situations that would behave differently if there were such a thing as ESP: What about the stock market? military secrets? multiple choice exams? The list is endless.

What we have done in this section is to explore the implications of some idea, in this case, the existence of ESP. Scientists do this all the time: If frustration causes aggression, then students who have been led to expect an A grade will get angry if they get a B, whereas they won't if they were expecting a B all along. Exploring what the implications of the existence of ESP and related phenomena would be make it highly implausible that they do exist. Too many ordinary things about our world would not be the case.

Exercise: Try to think of the implications on the military if there were such a thing as ESP, psychokinesis, or precognition.

Section 26

Why Are Psychologists So Skeptical?

Principle: Skepticism is not a dirty word. It's an attitude that is
needed in both science and ordinary life.

It frequently happens when I am discussing some controversial topic
such as ESP that my listener will ask, "Why are you so skeptical?" This
question might be followed by the statement, "But I was taught that..."

To many people a skeptic is one who doesn't believe anything, particularly when it comes to religion. Certainly that describes some skeptics, and
even some psychologists.

But that is not what we are talking about here. We are concerned with
the role of skepticism in science. It is helpful to know the origin of the word
skeptic, which comes from the Greek word, *skeptikos,* meaning to consider
thoughtfully. A skeptic is one who is willing to consider claims to truth
thoughtfully; who asks for the terms in a discussion to be defined clearly;
who looks for logical consistency in a proposition; who requires evidence
before believing something.

Suppose you are walking down the street in a city and a stranger
walks up to you and holds out a small box containing a watch. If he tells
you it is a genuine Rolex, but he will sell it to you for $25, you would proba-
bly be a little skeptical. You might suspect either that it is a cheap imitation
or that it has been stolen. In either case, you would remember what your
grandmother told you: "If it sounds too good to be true, it probably is."

You might object that this isn't skepticism; it's just plain common
sense. The kind of skepticism we are talking about is very much like common sense. When we are considering a used car in a dealer's lot and the

61

salesperson says it has had easy use, we ask what he means by easy use. (We ask him to define terms.) If he says it has had regular maintenance, we ask to see the service records. (We look for evidence that bears on the claim.) If he says it has never been in a wreck, we check to see if it has been repainted. (We look for logical consistency.)

Someone who does these things while shopping for a used car is considered smart. We should be just as smart when our teachers tell about psychology, or any other subject. True, our teachers are generally more reliable than the stereotype of a used car salesman. But good students are the ones who apply the same skeptical skills to the ideas they are being sold in college that they apply to a used car salesperson's pitch.

Exercise: Discuss how too little or too much skepticism could both be undesirable on ordinary life situations. Compare the effects of varying degrees of skepticism with those of love, generosity, and other feelings.

Section 27

How Do You Explain Déjà Vu?

Principle: *When something seems mysterious, try to explain it in terms of a scientific principle that is already known.*

Déjà vu is the strange sensation we all have from time to time that something we are experiencing right now has happened to us before, together with the realization that this sensation cannot be true. It may happen when we are taking a test, meeting a blind date, or having a job interview—situations that have considerable significance for us. The *déjà vu* experience tends to have a strong emotional component that makes it stand out in our experience and tempts us to give it a paranormal explanation.

Many authors have noted the *déjà vu* experience, from St. Augustine through Charles Dickens and Marcel Proust up to the present day. And many explanations of the strange phenomenon have been proposed (Sno & Linszen, 1990). Some have suggested that it is the result of the two hemispheres of the brain acting slightly out of synchrony; Freud thought it was a kind of defense mechanism; even holographic explanations have been offered. But many others have fallen back on paranormal explanations: reincarnation, soul travel, and the like. Suffice it to say that very little evidence exists to support any of these notions.

But let's step back and do something that scientists find basic to studying a new problem: Let's ask whether this experience can be explained by something we know already.

A little reflection will reveal that, whatever *déjà vu* is, it is an error of memory. And one thing we know about memory is that it isn't perfect—we all have wished our memories were perfect when we were taking a test or trying to remember someone's name.

First, we should note that we have so many experiences in a lifetime that it is rare when we see something totally new to us. Most rooms have four walls, a floor, and a ceiling. Even social situations tend to be stereotyped. Suppose you are in the middle of an argument with someone. Under the emotional stress of the moment, we tend to engage in exchanges of the "So's your old man"—"You're one, too" type; not exactly creative. These are the sorts of situations in which we tend to have the strong feeling that we have been there before—we have.

And even if we haven't experienced a situation directly, consider the amount of vicarious experiences we obtain from reading, television, and the like. You have probably had the experience of watching a TV show for a few minutes and then realizing that you have seen it many years before. Considering the amount of reading and television we engage in, it would be hard to imagine an experience that is totally new to us. Thus, many situations could seem to be old and new at the same time because they are very similar to an old experience.

So, realizing that new situations may be similar to old ones, let's consider some of the difficulties we face every day. Suppose you are at a party, and an attractive person comes up and says, "Hi, remember me? We met last year at Craig's party!" You scratch your head and try to decide if you really did meet her, or if this is a pickup line. Let's analyze the possibilities.

Now either you did meet her before, or you didn't. And you either remember her or you don't. This provides us with a two-by-two matrix of possibilities, as we see in the table that follows.

HAVE YOU MET BEFORE?

Do you remember?	Yes	No
Yes	You remember her (ordinary memory)	You think you remember her (*déjà vu*)
No	You don't remember her (ordinary forgetting)	You don't remember her (ordinary memory)

You are not surprised when you remember someone you have met before (upper left cell of the matrix). Nor are you surprised when you realize you haven't met someone before (lower right cell). Alas, you are all too familiar with the case where you can't remember someone you met last year at a party. You chalk it up to *forgetting,* and realize it is a failure of memory.

Why, then, should we be surprised when we see a new face and think it is an old one? If we realize that our memory can fail by not recognizing something that is actually old, why can't our memory fail in the opposite way? In other words, if we accept false negatives (forgetting an old face), why can't we accept false positives (thinking we remember a new face)?

But *déjà vu* bothers us because the knowledge that we couldn't possibly have experienced this before comes along with a strong feeling that we did. Here we must introduce another idea: Our degree of certainty about a memory is not a perfect measure of its truth. Usually we are reasonably sure that we know or don't know something. But there are times when we are positive we know something we don't. Many experiments could be cited that demonstrate this point.

A theory known as *signal detection theory* demonstrates that although there is a correlation between our certainty and the truth of the matter that we remember (or don't remember) something, the correlation is far from perfect. Sometimes when we are positive that we remember something, we don't, and vice versa.

But let's take an everyday example. Suppose you have lost your keys, and you ask your roommate if she has seen them. You may say that you are positive you put them in your purse. She may be equally positive that she saw you putting them on the desk. You may each suspect the other of taking them. (This is a familiar scene in nursing homes, sadly.) Eventually, after much searching, and perhaps some unpleasantness, you find the keys in the pocket of your jeans, where you no doubt left them.

To repeat, our certainty about the truth of some memories (and lots of other things as well) is not infallible proof of the facts of the matter.

These two notions, that *déjà vu* is an error of memory and that we can be wrong about things we believe, take the mystery out of *déjà vu*. We have taken something that we didn't understand and found a way of understanding it in terms of something else that we do understand. This is a fundamental characteristic of the way scientists work. (But it still seems spooky when it happens—although, we hope, less so than before.)

Exercise: Reports of flying saucers have been explained as various phenomena associated with ordinary vision. One of the characteristics attributed to flying saucers is their supposed ability to stop and start instantaneously without taking time to accelerate the way an airplane would. Look up *saccadic eye movements* in a perception book (or even in a dictionary, under *saccade*) and show how they could explain this phenomenon.

Section 28

Wasn't Hypnosis Once Considered a Pseudoscience?

Principle: One of the main features of science is that it progresses.
Just because something like hypnosis eventually
developed into a science doesn't mean than all areas now
considered pseudosciences will do the same.

Students who have heard me say that ESP is a pseudoscience sometimes ask, "But wasn't hypnosis once considered a pseudoscience?" The
implication is that I should take ESP seriously because it might become a
science some day.

The idea that we should take pseudosciences seriously because there
might be some validity to them has been called the *Fulton-non-sequitur:*
They laughed at Fulton when he put a steam engine in a boat, and look
what happened.

The list of things that scientists have scoffed at is quite long and provides grist for the mill of people who want to point out human fallibility,
and scientific fallibility in particular. You may have heard of the "fact" that
scientists once proved that a bumblebee can't fly. This story has some basis
in fact. *One* scientist *once* thought he had proven mathematically that it was
impossible for bees to fly, but that was only one scientist, and he was, plain-
ly, wrong. Nevertheless, the story gets repeated because it is a good story,
after all.

More significant are cases where scientists have changed their minds
about important things. Scientists once believed that "stones do not fall
from the sky" (see Section 24). But now we know quite a lot about mete-

orites. Among the more amusing notions that scientists once believed is that geese hibernate under water.

But hypnosis is an excellent example in psychology that illustrates the way scientists change their minds. Franz Anton Mesmer was a eighteenth-century Viennese physician who believed that the heavenly bodies influence human lives by means of magnetism, which had been recently discovered. He held sessions much like séances in which he dressed up in a magician's robe and passed magnets over people's bodies while suggesting that they would be healed. People fell into trances, and many were healed of their illnesses.

Understandably, this caught the attention of the authorities, and Mesmer felt it wise to leave Vienna for Paris. There he was no less controversial, and a commission of the French government, headed by Benjamin Franklin, who was the U.S. ambassador to France, concluded that the cures had nothing to do with magnetism. Mesmer was discredited and retired to Austria in disgrace.

Nevertheless, many scientists continued to be interested in the phenomenon, which was eventually named *hypnotism* because of the similarity of some of its typical effects to sleep. Over the years, scientists have come to realize that hypnosis is an exaggerated form of the suggestibility that all persons demonstrate. Thus, although it still can seem pretty weird to watch a person perform under hypnotic suggestion, scientists have a reasonably good understanding of how the phenomenon works. (To be sure, there are still a fairly large number of people with little scientific training who make some unscientific claims about hypnosis.)

The fact that scientists frequently change their minds is actually one of the great strengths of science, not a weakness. As a result of these changes, science progresses. If you see a field of study that hasn't changed in many years, then you have something that isn't science. Recall that Mesmer believed that the heavenly bodies influence people's lives. In other words, he believed in astrology. One characteristic of astrology is that its charts and predictions haven't changed in thousands of years—in spite of tremendous advances in our knowledge of the heavens. No true science has remained unchanged during that time, or even a much shorter period.

So the next time someone says to you, "What do scientists know? They're always changing their minds!" simply ask, "Would you prefer that they never learned anything new?"

Exercise: Think of something you have read about recently or heard on the news that made scientists change their minds.

Section 29

Why Do Psychologists Study Such Artificial Situations?

Principle: *Artificial situations provide the opportunity for scientists to observe phenomena in their purest form.*

I recall vividly the first departmental party I attended as a new graduate student, when I was just beginning to learn how a psychologist was supposed to act. The discussion turned to the work of B. F. Skinner, who at the time was at the peak of his career. One of the faculty members, having had several martinis, climbed unsteadily onto a chair. Holding his drink in one hand and gesturing with the other, he barely maintained his balance as he declaimed on what he perceived as the triviality of Skinner's work: "When you put a rat in a little box with nothing in it but a lever to press, how on earth can it do anything of the slightest psychological interest? We need more natural research settings!" If I told you the professor's name, you wouldn't recognize it. Skinner, on the other hand, is generally considered one of the all-time giants of psychology.

Experimental situations are often artificial precisely for the purpose of discovering the principles of behavior in as pure a form as possible, uncontaminated by the real world. Once the principles are understood, then they can be applied in many different situations. The principles discovered by Skinner and others using rats in Skinner boxes have had a tremendous impact on psychology and everyday life, from timeouts in childrearing to computer-aided instruction.

I could give many other examples. I remember also as a graduate student thinking that much of the work on human learning that was being done at the time was boring in the extreme. In those days squadrons of psychologists studied how people learned nonsense syllables, such as BAZ and ZIK, that were presented one at a time on little machines called memory drums. Memory drum research has gone the way of hula hoops, but the principles learned from it help us to understand why we remember better the material that comes at both the beginning and the end of lectures, poems, music, and lists of names than we can the stuff in the middle. The so-called *serial position effect* is one of the hardiest findings in psychology, and it was studied using the most artificial of settings.

Douglas Mook (1983) has argued that the artificiality of research settings permits us to understand phenomena in their purest form and gives us a basis then to apply the principles learned to the real world.

Exercise: Think of a standard experimental situation in biology, chemistry, or physics. How much does it resemble "real life"?

Section 30

How Does the Rat Understand That Pressing the Bar Gets It Food?

Principle: *Occam's razor teaches us that it is important not to assume that learning involves awareness.*

Many people find it perfectly obvious that when something is learned by an animal or human, the learner is aware of what has been learned. They believe that when we understand something, we know that we know it and can explain it in words. We will soon see that the situation is not as simple as this. But first we must discuss why scientists sometimes seem to question the obvious.

As long ago as the fourteenth century, a monk named William of Occam suggested that explanations should be as simple as possible and should not assume any more than is necessary. This principle, known as *Occam's razor*, has become a major tenet of science. In the case of learning, Occam's razor suggests that we should not be too quick to assume that conscious awareness is involved in learning.

Because it is hard to know what rats are conscious of, we will discuss an experiment in which humans were operantly conditioned in a manner essentially the same way rats are. Many years ago, Ralph Hefferline and others hooked up human subjects to electrodes connected to various parts of their body (Hefferline, Keenan & Harford, 1959). They told the subjects their job was to turn off an irritating noise, but they weren't told how they were supposed to do it. By the end of the experiment, the subjects had learned to turn off the noise, but they did not become aware of exactly how they had done it.

Some of the subjects thought they had done it by making various odd movements of their body, but none of them figured it out, even though they had been successful in doing it. In fact, the response was a thumb twitch so small they could not even make it on purpose. This experiment strongly implies that awareness is not necessary for learning to take place.

Going back to animals, the usual procedure for teaching rats to press the bar, or pigeons to peck the key, is to reward them for closer and closer approximations of the desired response. This procedure is called *shaping*. Because shaping requires a considerable amount of the experimenter's time, *autoshaping* is commonly used instead. Autoshaping involves putting the animal in the Skinner box and leaving it there until it learns the response on its own, without any intervention by the experimenter. This is slower than the usual shaping procedure, but it saves the experimenter's time.

One experimenter of my acquaintance had trained his rats by autoshaping and was using them in some experiment. It was his habit to put the rat in the Skinner box, go away, and come back when the session was over without staying around to watch the rats, which can be pretty boring.

After one session he noticed that a rat had a sore on its head, so he put some ointment on it before putting it back in its cage, not thinking much about it. The next day, as he put the rat in the Skinner box, he saw that the sore had begun to heal, but after the session he noticed that it had gotten worse again. Curious about to what was causing the sore, the next time he put the rat in the Skinner box he watched what it was doing. Unlike all the other rats, this one had not learned to press the bar with its paws, but had propped itself upside down against the wall of the box with its tail in the air, and was pushing the bar with its head.

Another incident involves pigeons. In a similar setup a pigeon was supposed to learn to peck a key for food. Now pigeons normally peck at a rather fast rate, but one bird was pecking only once every few seconds. When the experimenter looked in, he discovered that the pigeon was backing up to the end of the cage, running and throwing itself at the key, and pushing it with its body.

These anecdotes illustrate, I think, why we should not assume that those animals were particularly aware of what actually caused the food to appear.

Returning to humans, there is considerable evidence that people learn many things without being aware of it (Seger, 1994). In contrast to the Hefferline study, recent work tends to involve learning of complex information, such as puzzles and motor tasks. This area of research has come to be known as *implicit learning*.

We need to be clear at this point that I am *not* arguing that learning is some mechanical process of stamping in stimulus-response associations.

Modern theories of learning and conditioning make use of concepts such as *expectancies, cognitive maps,* and the like. What I am arguing is that we should not immediately assume that these terms imply that when something is learned, the learner is aware of what has been learned. Occam's razor teaches us that we should use concepts such as expectancies only when they are needed, and that we should not assume that an expectancy for a rat is the same thing it is for us in everyday life.

> **Exercise:** Immediately after they give birth, female cats lick their kittens dry and eat the placenta. Some people might think that the cat knows that the kittens need to get warm and that the placenta would be a source of contamination if it weren't disposed of. What possible explanations for the mother cat's behavior might you think of by applying Occam's razor?

Section 31

How Could That Be a Coincidence? (Part 1)

Principle: In order for two events to be considered a coincidence, we have to notice something about them first.

We are often struck by events that seem too unlikely to have occurred by chance. We may dream about someone the same night she dies. We may find that two identical twins separated at birth both married women named Jennifer, both drive Chevrolets, and both dislike mustard. Events like these lead many people to believe in the paranormal. I have had many people relate stories like this and say, "How could that possibly be a coincidence? It's just too unlikely!"

First, we need to clarify what we mean by a coincidence. Two statisticians, Perci Diaconis and Fred Mosteller (1989), have defined a coincidence as "a surprising concurrence of events, perceived as meaningfully related, with no apparent causal connection" (p. 853). Note the words, *surprising, perceived, meaningful,* and *apparent.* These are all psychological terms, which indicates that understanding coincidences involves psychology as much as statistics. Untold numbers of unlikely events occur every day that do not strike us as surprising and so do not get considered coincidences.

One of my favorite coincidences happened when I was riding in the back seat of my father's car as his friend in the front seat tried to think of the name of someone he had known years before. Just then my father stopped at a traffic light in town, next to a bank that had a large clock out front. "That's it!" the man exclaimed, "Hagman! It's written right there on the clock!"

Now Hagman is an unusual name. There are no Hagmans in the Greater Pittsburgh Telephone Directory, and only three Hagemans and two Hagemanns, out of two-thirds of a million listings. And I have never seen a Hagman clock before or since. This story illustrates all of Diaconis and Mosteller's criteria for a coincidence: We were all surprised (amazed, actually); we perceived the event as meaningful because the man was trying to think of the name; and we couldn't think of any possible causal connection between seeing the name and trying to think of it.

But untold numbers of unlikely events happen together each day that we ignore. The Pennsylvania daily number yesterday was 217 and the one for Ohio was 780. Each one has a one in 1000 chance of occurring, and the probability that precisely those two numbers would come up together is one in a million. But there is no obvious connection between them, and besides it was 100% certain that two three-digit numbers had to come up, so there is no apparent coincidence.

Exercise: Ask someone to recall a striking coincidence that he or she personally experienced. Can you identify what made the incident seem significant?

Section 32

How Could That Be a Coincidence? (Part 2)

Principle: *It is easier to find coincidences if you shoot the arrow first and draw the bull's eye later.*

If you look hard enough, you will begin to see coincidences everywhere. This is the principle behind the practice of numerology, which is an attempt to find meanings in numbers. One of my favorite examples of numerology is the claim that William Shakespeare was the translator of the King James Bible. The "proof" is that in the King James Bible the 46th word of Psalm 46 is "shake" and the 46th word from the end is "spear." Why 46? Shakespeare was 46 years old when the King James Bible was published.

Numerology requires a certain cleverness and a willingness to spend hours going through data until something apparently meaningful pops out. I admire people who have the patience to do it. Some of the best examples have been given by Martin Gardner, who is responsible for the one about Shakespeare. But numerologists never specify in advance exactly where they will find a meaningful coincidence. An interesting example is given by the sometimes popular activity of "proving" that a certain person is the Beast of Revelation, whose number is 666. For examples, it has been noticed that Ronald Wilson Reagan had three names, each having six letters. Ergo, Ronald Reagan is the Beast of Revelation. But it has been "proven" that many other people are the Beast by using a variety of other methods, such as giving values to the letters in a name (A = 1, B = 2, etc.) and finding that they add up to 666, and so forth. Because there is no end to the possibilities, almost anyone can be "proven" to be the Beast.

The same method used in numerology when applied to psychological data has been called *data dredging,* or *data snooping.* If you look at a set of data enough different ways you will eventually find something that looks interesting. To be more specific, if you perform a statistical test on any large set of completely random data, you will get an apparently significant result 5% of the time, using typical criteria. And if you do another independent test on the same data, you have the same 5% chance of finding significance. So if you do enough tests, all different, on the same data, you are bound to find something significant, even if all the data are perfectly random.

If you perform 14 independent tests on a set of random data, you have better than an even chance of finding something "significant." If you do 20 tests, your chances are almost two out of three.

Many psychologists as well as numerologists are guilty now and then of data dredging, which is the equivalent of shooting the arrow first and drawing the bull's eye later. This is the reason that it is common to make a distinction between *exploratory* and *confirmatory* data analysis. Exploratory data analysis is done when a researcher looks through a set of data for an interesting pattern that doesn't seem to be the result of chance. Exploratory analysis is done without predicting in advance exactly what one is looking for. Because of the danger of data dredging, with its effects on statistical significance, however, psychologists know they should repeat any test that shows a significant finding, whenever they happen to stumble upon it unexpectedly in a set of data. They should do another experiment, or another independent analysis, which they have specified in advance, to confirm what they found by exploratory analysis.

When my wife was a little girl, she thought it would be nice to have a magic rock that would find treasures when she tossed it at random. She picked up a likely candidate and gave it a good heave. Running over to it, she was amazed and delighted to see that it had landed on a quarter, enough in those days to buy a ticket to a double feature at the movies with a nickel left over for Good 'n Plenties. As you can imagine, she tried over and over again to find treasure with that rock. As you can also imagine, it never again landed on anything more valuable than dirt and grass. But her method was scientific. She first tested her hypothesis by exploratory data analysis: "Maybe if I throw this rock, it will find treasure." But then she went on to confirmatory data analysis: "Will it do it again?"

Numerologists have the luxury of stopping with exploratory data analysis, but psychologists need to follow up with confirmatory analysis.

Exercise: Take the most recent winning daily lottery number you can find. Find a connection between that number and some other number in your life, such as birthday, telephone number, and the like. What is the essential difference between doing that and predicting what tomorrow's number will be?

Section 33

How Could That Be a Coincidence? (Part 3)

Principle: *Evaluation of probability is a technical matter that cannot be done without study.*

Suppose you and a friend were going to take a trip by airplane. While you were at the gate waiting to board the plane, your friend looks out the window at the plane and says, "Hey! There is no way that thing can fly. The wings are too small, and there aren't enough engines." You would probably laugh and point out that the plane obviously flew to the airport, unless it was built on the spot. But you might also note that unless a person is an engineer and has done the necessary calculations, he or she has no right to an opinion on whether the plane can fly or not.

This should seem obvious enough. But people say something like the following to me all the time: "There is no way it could have been chance that I dreamed about Aunt Lillian the night before she died." But probability is a technical matter, and it requires considerable training and work before the chance of various events can be determined. Why do we think we can do it intuitively? Some events are much more likely than they would seem.

The standard example is the famous birthday problem: How many people would you have to have in a room before it would be an even bet that two of them would have been born on the same day of the same month (e.g., November 11)? I have asked many classes this question, and the typical guess is around 100. The fact is that it requires only 23. By the time you have 50 people in a room, it is a virtual certainty that two will have the same birthday.

Not everything turns out to be more likely than it seems intuitively. Suppose there were a hospital that had exactly seven births per week that were randomly spaced over days. How many weeks would have to go by before it was an even bet that there would be exactly one birth on each of the seven days in the week? The answer is more than three years!

So because we can't guess probabilities, I have done some simple calculations to estimate what the probability is of thinking of Aunt Lillian the night she dies. Without going into details, it turns out that this sort of event should happen to at least six people in the greater Pittsburgh metropolitan area (approximately 2,500,000 people) every day. No wonder strange things seem to happen to us. And they do seem strange when they happen. But without doing the calculations, we have no right to say that it couldn't have been chance.

Finally, even if the odds of some event were extremely small, it could still happen by chance. The odds of any six-digit number being drawn at random is one in a billion. But if you draw a six-digit number, one of those one-in-a-billion numbers is bound to come up. So even extremely rare events happen. They have to.

> **Exercise:** Because the point to this unit is that probability is technical, any exercise must be very basic. For example, what is the probability of flipping a coin and getting three heads in a row? Consider that each flip of a coin is independent. The simplest way of getting the answer is to list all possible outcomes of tossing a coin three times: HHH, HHT, and so on. Because it is the case that each outcome is equally likely, the probability is found by dividing the number of outcomes that meet your criterion for success (here there is only one: HHH) by all possible outcomes. So the key is to list all the possibilities. The answer is 1 divided by the total number of possibilities. Then what is the probability of getting at least two heads?
>
> (Answers: 1/8, 1/2)

Section 34

Can We Hear Satanic Messages in Music That Is Played Backward?

Principle: *We test hypotheses not by trying to confirm them, but by comparing them to rival explanations.*

In 1990, the heavy metal band Judas Priest was sued when a pair of teenagers committed suicide after doing drugs and alcohol while listening to the album *Stained Class.* This is perhaps the most famous manifestation of the widespread belief that record companies put Satanic messages in music that can be heard when it is played backward.

It happens to be true that people will hear messages in musical and nonmusical speech that is played backward. When John Vokey and Don Read (1985) played popular musical numbers backward, they found that people did, in fact, hear meaningful words. For example, when Queen's song "Another One Bites the Dust" is played backward, many people hear the message, "It's fun to smoke marijuana." I have played this number backward to my classes many times, and all hear this "message," especially when I suggest what they should listen for.

Does this prove the claim? Not quite. People also heard intelligible messages when Vokey and Read played the 23rd Psalm and Lewis Carroll's poem "Jabberwocky" backward. Most people would consider it highly unlikely that the Bible contains hidden Satanic messages. And "Jabberwocky" presents an interesting case, because it consists of nonsense words when listened to *forward*. It strains the imagination to suppose that Lewis Carroll would say to himself, "suppose that someday there will be a machine that can record words and play them backward. I think I'll write a poem that will be nonsense when listened to normally, but will say 'Saw a girl with a weasel in her mouth' when played backward."

The fact is, we hear meaningful utterances in virtually *any* words played backward. We can't help it. It is a manifestation of our tendency to make sense out of meaningless input. Remember seeing animals in the clouds when you were a child? *Backmasking* is the auditory equivalent. When we listen to words played backward they become meaningless—the actual words cannot be understood, but our ear makes sense out of the nonsense sounds anyway, even though they have nothing to do with the original (forward) message.

A number of principles are illustrated in this example. In Section 32 we discussed the dangers of data dredging. Listening to records backward is an example of data dredging because no specific message is predicted in advance—the listener just tries to find something. A second principle illustrated by backmasking is that one should try first to explain the unknown on the basis of the known, as we discussed in Section 27.

But a new principle here is that we test hypotheses by comparing them to rival hypotheses, not by trying to prove them correct: Which is more plausible, Satanic messages placed in passages in religious texts written before recording technology existed or the well-known tendency to construct meaning from random stimuli?

> **Exercise:** Suppose you discovered that some recording studios actually did put backward messages in their music. How would you answer someone who said, "Well, they wouldn't do it if it didn't work, would they?" Hint: Think of an alternative reason why they might.

Section 35

I Found This Great Self-Help Book!

Principle: *Nature is typically more complicated that any one theory can account for.*

"Professor, your lectures are so complicated that I decided to look in the bookstore, and I found this great book that explains everything!" Usually the person who says this to me is an eager student who is trying hard to learn the material in the course but is finding the textbook and lectures frustrating.

Self-help books form an amazingly large proportion of the psychology section of most bookstores, and they exist in great variety. Some contain mostly unscientific or antiscientific ideas based on astrology, witchcraft, magic, and the like. I am not particularly concerned with those here, although many others mix scientific and unscientific ideas together and some claim the name of psychology because it seems to add some measure of credibility to their notions.

But self-help books tend to share one characteristic that is of interest to us here: One basic idea underlies the book, and it is usually apparent from the title. *I'm OK, You're OK,* by Thomas Harris, is a classic, and *Men Are from Mars, Women Are from Venus,* by John Gray, is a recent example. Further, they tend to offer a simple solution to a problem: *Get Rid of Him,* by Joyce Vedral, or they promise a great deal: *The Sky's the Limit,* by Wayne Dyer.

Some appear more sophisticated by offering a numbered list of suggestions: *Ten Stupid Things Women Do To Mess Up Their Lives,* by Laura Schlessinger; or *Seven Habits of Highly Effective People,* by Stephen Covey.

All self-help books have one thing in common: They oversimplify. They take an idea, or a few ideas, and they package them in a way that the average person can understand and will want to read. In the process, it is inevitable that the material will be oversimplified. Alternative points of view will not be considered. Complications will be overlooked. Problems that might result from following the advice won't be mentioned. If they were, we would have a textbook, or worse, an encyclopedia, and few people would read it (or, more important, buy it).

Self-help books often contradict each other. The massively popular *I'm OK, You're OK* advises us to act on the rational "adult" part of our personality, and to avoid the dependent "child" or judgmental "parent" mode. By contrast, self-help books in the recovery tradition, based on the model of Alcoholics Anonymous, tell us that we are victims and that we need to surrender our wills to a higher power. It should be obvious that these ideas are contradictory.

Don't get me wrong. These books often contain useful information, and sometimes people can be helped by following their advice. Many therapists recommend self-help books in conjunction with therapy, or even in place of it. And there is some evidence that they can be helpful when used thoughtfully.

But the very fact that they must oversimplify means that they can be misleading. No author can predict all the situations in which all readers will find themselves, nor anticipate the myriad ways in which readers will misunderstand what they are trying to say. And people who follow the advice can get hurt, if they don't use common sense or get advice from a wise friend or a professional counselor.

The problem is: The world is not as simple as the self-help books tend to suggest. The solution to one person's problem may be exactly the cause of another's: One person might be too rational and not be in touch with her feelings; another might be depending too much on emotion and not be using his head enough. That's why textbooks generally give such complicated explanations for any phenomenon and usually discuss pros and cons of any theory.

Here is a rule that most psychologists would agree with: If you think you have found the answer to all your problems, you're almost certainly wrong.

Exercise: Get a self-help book out of the library. Compare it to the motivation chapter of your textbook. Does the self-help book qualify its claims or suggest special circumstances under which its advice would not be appropriate?

Section 36

How Can Psychology Be a Science When Every Person Is Unique?

Principle: Science studies things that individuals have in common.

One of the amazing facts of the human condition is that each of us is genetically unique. Except for identical twins, the probability that two siblings will have all the same genes is so vanishingly small that it is essentially zero. Even identical twins, who share all the same genetic material and have much of their environment in common, have unique experiences. Somehow many people find this uniqueness very significant. Personality chapters in psychology books often emphasize how each individual is different from every other individual.

Let's accept the fact that we are all unique. Does that make it impossible for psychology to be a science? Or does it mean that psychology is a special kind of science that has to take our uniqueness into account?

From the standpoint of psychology, the question is whether the things that make each of us unique make any difference for our particular scientific purpose. Let's go back to biology for a moment. Even though every human individual—except for the rare identical twin—is genetically unique, the science of genetics is flourishing today. We read constantly about new means of treating hereditary diseases with genetic alterations, for example. The reason geneticists can do this work is because even unique genetic material is made up of simple components that are the same in all individuals.

Many psychological processes, such as the ability to adapt to seeing in low light, perceiving the direction of a sound source, learning to search for a vowel among a set of letters, and so forth—obey the same laws in just about any person. For the most part, psychologists assume that psychological processes work pretty much the same in all people. It is assumed that curly-headed people see the same as straight-haired people, and dark-skinned people hear the same as light-skinned people. Similarly, physicists assume that either black or white balls respond to the force of gravity the same way.

Of course, some dimensions on which people differ do make a difference in their behavior. Light-skinned people do see somewhat differently than dark-skinned people because they have less of a certain pigment in their eyes that blocks out particular kinds of light rays. This does not surprise us. We have simply found another dimension that must be considered when making lawful statements about people. Our physicist might not pay attention to the color of the balls when doing a study of the effects of gravity but would be very interested in their color if she were studying how fast they warmed up under a heat lamp. Then their color would be an important thing to pay attention to.

What we have been describing so far is called the *nomothetic* approach to science, which emphasizes the function of universal laws. We should note that some psychologists have argued for the *idiographic* approach, which says that human behavior is so entangled in the particular life histories of individuals that it is impossible to take the nomothetic approach. The idiographic approach looks for explanations in the unique situation of the individual. This approach is most commonly taken in areas of psychology such as social and personality psychology.

Whether the nomothetic approach is always appropriate is not the point, however. We simply want to argue that uniqueness of individuals does not rule out the making of general laws of behavior that apply to all. Most of what is found in psychology books is based on the successful application of the assumption that laws of behavior, like the laws of genetics, apply to everyone in spite of our uniqueness.

Exercise: Think of three principles in psychology that apply to all individuals.

Section 37

How Do Biorhythms Work?

Principle: *The processes that control human behavior are subject to variability.*

Biorhythm theory says that human behavior is controlled by the interaction of three cycles: a 23-day masculine, or physical, cycle; a 28-feminine, or emotional, cycle; and a 31-day intellectual cycle. Performance in the respective domains is supposed to be best during the up half of the cycle and worst during the down half. However, days on which a cycle is shifting from positive to negative are considered critical days. Because two or three cycles sometimes overlap, there can be double or triple critical days, and days when two or three cycles are simultaneously positive or negative (Hines, 1979).

Suffice it to say that the whole notion of biorhythm theory is pseudoscience: The physical and emotional cycles were dreamed up by Wilhelm Fliess on the basis of numerology rather than scientific evidence (Gardner, 1976). The intellectual cycle was added later. Although biorhythm theory has been popular for many years, scientific tests have not substantiated it (Hines, 1979). Nevertheless, it remains popular among people who are more impressed by anecdotes than scientific evidence.

We need to be careful to distinguish biorhythms from *biological rhythms,* also known as chronobiology. Whereas the former is a pseudoscience, the latter is a vigorous area of genuine science. It is well-known that many different rhythms are found in biological systems, including humans. We are familiar with the daily cycle of sleep and wakefulness and the roughly 28-day menstrual cycle. In addition, a host of organs and systems of the body have cycles, including heart rate, body temperature, urine output, and so on. These are the cycles that get out of whack when we experience jet lag. Part of the distress we feel is the result of the various cycles readjusting to the new time zone at different rates. Thus, we might be wide awake but not hungry; or sleepy when our kidneys are working the hardest. We are not questioning the validity of biological rhythms.

Why, then, are we so against biorhythms? Isn't it enough to say that there is no evidence for them? The reason biorhythm theory is particularly misguided is that it shares some of the properties of astrology, which is essentially a system of magic (see Section 38). As with astrology, the date of birth is critical. Astrology emphasizes the location of the planets at the time of birth. Biorhythm theory claims that birth supposedly triggers the three cycles.

Granted, the moment of birth is pretty critical for a baby, but there is no particular reason to assume that these three cycles should be triggered at birth. Why not before? Why not by the first sunrise?

But more tellingly, all biological processes have a certain amount of variability built into them. In fact, our familiar sleep-waking cycle is known in biology as a *circadian* rhythm. The Greek roots for the word *circadian* mean "about a day." Many experiments have shown that the sleep-waking cycles of humans and animals who are deprived of cues to the actual time of day will tend to run 25 or more hours long (Wever, 1979). Additionally, women are well aware that the menstrual cycle is not exactly 28 days.

More than anything else, the reliance on birthdate as the basis of calculating biorhythms demonstrates that this theory is pseudoscience. Actual biological rhythms can be measured by physical means. The absence of a physical means of measurement (and hence a physical basis for their action) is a prime characteristic of magic. And measurement of actual biological rhythms demonstrate that they vary somewhat from cycle to cycle.

Exercise: Suppose that alertness, as measured by brain activity, is known to vary in a cycle of about 90 minutes. How would you go about testing a prediction that a person makes more mental errors at different phases of the cycle? How is this fundamentally different from testing the effect of biorhythms on performance?

Section 38

What about Astrology?

Principle: *All branches of science are related by interconnecting theoretical concepts. If a system of thought does not connect to the rest of science, it is almost certainly pseudoscience.*

Astrology is one of the most widely believed pseudopsychologies. Almost everyone knows his or her astrological sign, many daily papers carry astrology columns, and asking people their signs is a common conversation starter. But scientists almost universally consider it to be a pseudoscience.

There are many reasons why astrology is a pseudoscience (Bok & Jerome, 1975). For one thing, its charts and predictions haven't changed in thousands of years—in spite of tremendous advances in our knowledge of the heavens. Even the locations of the stars on which the system is based have changed in that time. So persons who believe themselves to be Capricorns are really Aquarians! Thus, astrology fails to meet one of the important criteria of science: that it progresses (see Section 28).

Another reason is that the predictions of astrology have been tested and found wanting. There have been any number of tests of personality, accomplishments, and other traits of people born under different signs, and they have consistently failed to confirm the predictions of astrology.

But the point we want to stress in this section is that the theoretical concepts of astrology have no connections with science. Scientists believe that science possesses a unity, the various sciences are but subsets, or branches, of one large science. The concepts of one branch of science should make connections with those of other branches.

But the concepts of astrology make no connections to other sciences. Consider the idea that the heavenly bodies exert influences on human behavior. A scientist immediately asks what form those influences take. What physical energy do they consist of? When we ask that, we have two likely candidate influences: gravitational and electromagnetic. It is a simple matter to calculate that the gravitational forces on a baby at birth emanating from the people in the delivery room far exceed the gravitational forces of the planets. Similarly, the electromagnetic energy from the light bulb over the delivery table vastly exceeds that coming from the heavens. So the known physical forces couldn't conceivably have any measurable effect on the baby.

Nor is there any known means by which gravitational or electromagnetic forces would have the types of effects on the baby that astrology claims. Thus, astrology fails to connect with any known principles of physics, physiology, or psychology. It just sits there all by itself.

Exercise: How does psychology relate to other sciences? Look in your textbook for connections between psychology and biology, anthropology, and sociology.

Section 39

Why Can't Psychologists Predict Who Will Commit a Violent Act?

Principle: *Prediction is often probabilistic.*

During the 1988 presidential campaign, supporters of George Bush used the infamous "Willie Horton" ad to help defeat Michael Dukakis. Willie Horton raped a woman while on furlough from a Massachusetts prison where he had been serving time for murder while Dukakis was governor of the state. We can be sure that Willie Horton had been judged unlikely to commit another crime before being released from prison.

This incident illustrates vividly the problem of predicting who will and who won't commit a violent act. In one legal proceeding after another, psychologists and psychiatrists are called on to testify whether a person is likely to commit another crime. And all too often we find that the psychologist for one side testifies that the person is harmless, and the psychologist for the other side testifies that he is another Willie Horton waiting to happen. How can psychology be scientific if psychologists can't agree on something so important as that?

The answer to this is, unfortunately, that we will probably never be able to predict exactly who will commit a violent crime and who won't. Human behavior is simply the result of too many variables to predict with great accuracy in any one case. We know with some degree of accuracy what percent of the population will commit murder. We can improve the prediction considerably by taking into account demographic variables, such as age, gender, education, income, and other factors. But the prediction inevitably becomes much less certain for the individual case.

The situation is rather similar to predicting the weather. We know the average weather for a given location. We can predict reasonably well the likelihood of rain for the next few days. But when it comes to predicting what will happen one month from now, we can't do much better than predicting the historical average. There simply are too many variables that enter into whether it will rain or not. The U.S. Weather Service uses gigantic computers and tons of data to predict the next day's weather. (And weather prediction is enormously more reliable than it was, say, 50 years ago.) But meteorologists still need to give the forecast in terms of probabilities, simply because of the enormous complexity of weather systems.

As unsatisfactory as this may be, it is the best we can do in many situations. A doctor has to advise a patient on whether to undergo a risky procedure based on probabilities. Government agencies make important decisions about the economy based on probabilistic models. To require psychology to do any better is to ask for the impossible.

Exercise: Think of a phenomenon in each of the following disciplines that cannot be predicted, except as a probability: geology, genetics, atomic physics.

Section 40

My Mother Went to a Psychologist Who Was No Help at All!

Principle: *People place too much weight on isolated cases and not enough on aggregate statistics. This tendency is known as the base rate fallacy.*

The following situation has probably happened to everyone who has just bought a new car. Someone you know will come up and say, "I'm looking for a new car. How do you like your new Whizzer?" Now your friend may really wonder how you could have bought a car that practically had "Dweebmobile" written all over it. But usually the person is genuinely trying to form an opinion on this particular new model.

Psychologists have found (Nisbett, Borgida, Crandall, & Reed, 1976) that the average person tends to place much more credence in individual data than in data that are based on a large number of cases. In the case of car buying, we take the opinions of our friend who may know nothing in particular about cars over the careful analysis of data from many owners by *Consumer Reports*. I have even had complete strangers stop me and ask how I like my car.

One reason for this phenomenon is certainly the vividness that a single case can convey. We can see our friend standing before us bragging about her new car, pleasure showing in her face, gestures, and tone of voice. By comparison, the pages of *Consumer Reports* or *Motor Trend* seem somewhat pale and lifeless. The vividness of individual cases is precisely why a U.S. President in the State of the Union speech will read a letter from a person who has been personally affected by his actions, or why I have used stories to illustrate points I am making in this book. We remember stories and are influenced by them more than by dry statistics. They are alive.

There is a good reason why we tend to be heavily influenced by personal experience. Imagine a hungry band of Pleistocene hunter-gatherers who come across a brilliant yellow frog they had never seen before. One of them picks it up, takes a bite out of it, and promptly falls over dead. Those people standing around who took that one experience to heart and never again touched yellow frogs had a greater likelihood of becoming our ancestors than those who kept an open mind until they took a survey to see how many people in neighboring tribes had ever dined on yellow frog. So we are predisposed to notice unusual events and draw conclusions on the basis of them in the absence of aggregate statistics, or repeatable observations. Once burnt, twice shy.

A side effect of this generally useful tendency is that we too often jump to general conclusions on the basis of individual data. We did not evolve to live in a technological world with computerized databases at our fingertips.

So when professors and others try to convince us of some psychological fact that does not fit with our own experience, we tend to be skeptical. It takes some effort to place our observations in a scientific context. But overcoming our tendency to draw conclusions from individual cases will make us better scientists and better purchasers of cars and psychological services.

Your mother should read the literature on the effectiveness of psychotherapy, where she will find that therapy is effective by and large but personal factors to some extent influence whether a particular client will benefit from a particular therapist.

> **Exercise:** Does your family usually drive a certain brand of car? How much does this preference depend on base-rate information about reliability, and other performance factors? How much does it depend on individual experiences, such as, "Uncle Joe once owned a Whizzer and it was in the shop every other week."

Section 41

Why Do Psychologists Avoid the Important Questions?

Principle: Science deals with questions that are answerable.

"What is man that thou art mindful of him?"
—Psalm 8

"What are people for?"
—Kurt Vonnegut

I once invited a believer in parapsychology to give a guest lecture in my course in pseudopsychology. He started out his talk by asking the class, "How many of you are concerned about the meaning of life?" Many hands went up. He continued, "Psychologists ignore questions of meaning, of spirituality, of ultimate values. Parapsychology is an attempt to study these important questions from a scientific point of view." Some of my students perked up considerably at this statement, hearing something they had been waiting for since the beginning of the course. Others looked at me out of the corner of their eye because I had dealt with that very issue in an earlier lecture.

My guest lecturer was illustrating vividly for my students one reason why parapsychology is a kind of pseudoscience: Science deals only with those questions that have empirical answers—those that we can pose in such a way that they can be answered by some objective evidence.

Some questions can't be answered because they involve value judgments: Are people inherently good or evil? What is the meaning of life? There are too many differences of opinion about what is good and what is evil. Others can't be answered because we don't have the technical ability right now to answer them: Could a computer imitate the human mind so well that we would consider it conscious?

It has been said that science substitutes unimportant questions that can be solved for important ones that cannot. Scientists work away on problems for which they can ask questions that seem to have empirical answers, for which they have the tools, on which they think they can make some progress. The rest they mostly ignore, not because these questions aren't important, but because they have nothing to say about them *as scientists*. These questions are left to philosophers, theologians, artists, and others to deal with.

Because I raised the matter of pseudoscience at the beginning of this section, I need to say that when philosophers and others deal with larger questions of life, they are not necessarily doing pseudoscience; they are doing philosophy, theology, art, and so forth. Pseudoscience is what happens when people try to use the methods of science on questions for which they are not suited. My guest was a pseudoscientist because he tried to bend the methods of science to questions that science can't answer. One clue to a pseudoscience is that there is a big gap between the concepts supposedly being studied and the methods employed to study them. How, for example, could you measure the meaning of life or the existence of an astral presence? Scientific questions have measurable answers: What is the effect of this drug on brain wave activity, or on the chemicals released at a particular kind of nerve synapse?

Of course, individual scientists have different opinions on which questions can be solved and which cannot, and whether a new technique gives us a basis for answering a question that was previously unanswerable. Thus we have differences of opinion on what line of work is science and what is pseudoscience. Some areas of research, such as work on altered states of consciousness, are a mixture of science and pseudoscience.

But you will probably wait in vain for a psychology instructor to spend much time on certain questions that are of great interest to you, because they are not the ones that science is designed to answer. On the other hand, I hope your instructor tells you many things that are completely fascinating.

Exercise: Which of the following questions seem to be scientific and which pseudoscientific?

1. What are the conditions under which people will demonstrate prejudice?
2. Is prejudice against people who are different from us undesirable?
3. What are the psychological functions of belief in life after death?
4. Is there life after death?

(Answer: Scientific: 1 and 3)

Section 42

Why Are So Many Criminals Let Off on the Basis of Insanity?

Principle: *We develop beliefs about the relative frequency of events based in part on their relative salience.*

In January 1994, Lorena Bobbitt, who had admitted to cutting off her husband's penis with a kitchen knife, was acquitted on the basis of temporary insanity. About a decade earlier, in 1982, President Reagan's would-be assassin, John Hinckley, was found not guilty by reason of insanity and was committed to a mental institution instead of to prison. These are only two of the high-profile cases in which the accused have used the insanity defense to escape prison.

Before we proceed any further, we need to note that *insanity* is not a psychological, or psychiatric, term, but a legal one. A psychologist might judge a person schizophrenic, or depressed, or whatever, but not insane. The concept of insanity has developed over the years as a way for the legal system to deal with people who cannot be held responsible for their actions. Although psychological considerations enter into the question, the concept is essentially legal. The latest version of the insanity defense is called the American Law Institute rule (American Law Institute, 1985), which says:

> A person is not responsible for criminal conduct if at the time of such conduct as a result of mental disease or defect he lacks substantial capacity either to appreciate the criminality [wrongfulness] of his conduct or to conform his conduct to the requirements of the law....The terms "mental disease or defect" do not include an abnormality manifested only by repeated criminal or otherwise antisocial conduct. (Part I. Article 4. Section 401, pp. 61–62)

So being declared legally insane is not the same thing as being mentally ill. Many more people would be diagnosed as having mental disease than would be judged insane. Further, a person can have varying degrees of mental illness, but that person is either sane or insane, just as he or she is either guilty or not guilty.

Many people believe that the insanity defense is used too often and that large numbers of guilty people are roaming the streets as a result. Is this the case?

It turns out that the insanity defense is actually very seldom used—between about one in 5000 and one in 200 arrests, depending on the state (Blau, McGinley, & Pasewark, 1993). Let's take .5% as the upper end of the range. That's way less than most people imagine the situation to be.

And that figure doesn't mean that the plea works: Something on the order of 10% of insanity pleas are successful. So it appears that less than .01% of people arrested for crimes get off on the basis of insanity.

Why, then, do we have the widespread belief that the insanity plea is used so often? The reason is that we form our impressions of the frequency of events in part by how noticeable, or salient, they are to us. When a Lorena Bobbitt or a John Hinckley is declared not guilty by reason of insanity, we pay a lot of attention because the deed they committed is so heinous. We may not even hear about the thousands of other cases where the plea is not made.

Even if the plea is made unsuccessfully, we don't seem to enter the fact into our informal probability calculations. How many people recall that Jeffrey Dahmer was unsuccessful in pleading insanity? (Serial killers rarely succeed with an insanity plea.)

The *differential salience* (how much things stand out, or get our attention) of events leads us to some rather bizarre beliefs. Many people will not fly because they believe it is unsafe, even though flying is many times safer on a per-mile basis than driving a car. The reason is simple: When a plane goes down, it makes the news, but car crashes rarely get the same attention. The fact is that the equivalent of a planeload of people die in car crashes every single day in the United States. But they die by the ones, twos, or threes, not by the hundreds, so it doesn't make the news. The result is that we get a biased idea of the relative safety of airplanes versus automobiles.

I had a friend who always planned his vacation to fall during the time of the full moon. He believed that the weather was always better then. It isn't. Believe me. (Or perhaps I should say that I am unaware of any evidence that the moon influences the weather, even though I have searched for it.) If you think about the difference in the salience of the combination of good weather and full moon compared to bad weather and full moon, you can see the basis of his erroneous belief. We have all looked up at a full moon in a clear sky and remarked on the beauty of the night. How many people have ever looked up at a sky full of clouds and rain and said? "Hey, what a rotten night for a full moon!"

Even a clear moonless night doesn't register in the same way because we don't tend to say, "Hey, Fred, what a beautiful night and there's no moon!" So of all the combinations—full moon/clear sky, full moon/cloudy sky, no moon/clear sky, no moon/cloudy sky—the only one that tends to register with us is full moon/clear sky. Thus, because of its greater salience, we tend to associate the full moon with good weather.

> **Exercise:** Show how differential salience can account for the widespread belief that more crimes, mental breakdowns, births, and so on happen at the time of the full moon.

> **Exercise:** Show how relative salience can account for racial stereotypes about crime rates.

Section 43

Why Are Psychologists So Liberal?

Principle: The fundamental attribution error leads people to underestimate the importance of situations in determining behavior.

It's true—at least in my experience: Psychologists are more liberal than the average person, or even the average college professor. To be sure, I actually know some psychologists who vote Republican and drive American cars, but the average psychologist I know tends to be relatively liberal. There may be a number of reasons this is so. For one thing, as a helping profession, psychology tends to attract people who want to improve the lot of their fellows.

But one reason psychologists tend to be more liberal may be that they are aware of certain biases in the way we think that cause people to underestimate the importance of the situation in determining behavior. It has been demonstrated many times that we tend to jump to the conclusion that a person's behavior reflects permanent personality characteristics rather than the demands of the situation.

Consider the following scenario: A husband comes downstairs in the morning, scowling. "Do I have any clean underwear?" he says.

"You can look downstairs in the laundry," she replies coldly.

"What's the matter? You're always grumpy in the morning."

"Only because you left your dirty underwear on the floor again. You never bother to put it in the hamper."

"That's because the hamper was down in the cellar. You always leave it down there. How can I put my dirty clothes away if there's no hamper?"

And so on.

You can see that both members of this fictitious couple attribute their own behavior to the situation (the partner's provocation), but attribute the partner's behavior to their stable, internal (personality) characteristics. This is, of course, a formula for endless strife.

This tendency to underestimate the importance of the situation and to overestimate the importance of permanent characteristics when attributing causes of another person's behavior has been called the *fundamental attribution error* (Ross, 1977). When we cut someone off in traffic, we tend to make the excuse for ourself that we are late or were forced to do it by the circumstances; when someone cuts us off, we decide he or she is a nasty person or a habitually bad driver.

The fact is, there are many situations in which we don't know why someone did something, whether it was the situation or the person. Further, there are times when both the situation and the person interact to cause a behavior. You may have heard an exasperated person say, "that's enough to make a preacher cuss." Ordinarily, we expect preachers to be examples of probity, but we realize that everyone has a personal limit.

A road I often drive has a sharp curve, and for a number of years cars would frequently run off the road and crash into a store that stood right next to the sidewalk. Eventually, the city decided to do something about it. What they did was erect a sturdy concrete barrier between the sidewalk and the store, ensuring that cars would crash into the barrier instead of the store. It wasn't long before the barrier was marred by gouges, paint, and rubber from the cars that crashed into it. Significantly, the city did not erect a sign that said, "Danger, Sharp Curve Ahead," or place reflective arrows to help motorists avoid the hazard.

This example of the fundamental attribution error is a classic case of "blaming the victim." The city could have attributed the crashes either to the unsafe conditions or to the drivers who were going too fast on the curved city street. By building the barrier, the city's engineers clearly showed that they attributed the crashes to the drivers and not the road. After all, we can hear them reason, thousands of people go past this spot without crashing—it's obviously the drivers' fault. But someone else could argue that the drivers who crashed had driven for thousands of miles without hitting anything—it must be the road.

This is but one instance of the argument that goes on constantly about automobile safety. The automobile industry resisted government-mandated safety devices for decades, arguing that car crashes were caused by the "nut behind the wheel." Nevertheless, as more and more safety features have been added to cars over the years and roads have been built to stricter safety standards, the accident rate has dropped dramatically. According to the *World Almanac* (1994), motor vehicle deaths rate per person decreased by

41% between 1970 and 1992. It would be hard to attribute that sharp drop entirely to changes in drivers.

As this is being written, Congress is debating a crime bill. Liberals and conservatives are arguing fiercely about the relative merits of spending money on prevention of crime versus building jails to lock up criminals. It should be obvious to everyone that committing a crime involves an interaction of causes involving both the individual and the situation. What we can't tell is how exactly what proportion of the crime rate is a consequence of which cause. Given that situation, it is no wonder that well-meaning people will come to different conclusions. And it should be no wonder that those who are familiar with the fundamental attribution error will tend more than others to lean more toward the situational causes of crime. Thus, it is no wonder that psychologists are more liberal than the general population.

Exercise: Show how different attitudes on the causes of poverty could be the result of the fundamental attribution error.

Section 44

Psychological Explanations Often Contradict Common Sense!

Principle: *Most problems have a simple answer that is obvious but wrong and a complicated answer that is counterintuitive but correct.*

Students often get frustrated at psychological explanations of some phenomenon, because to them the truth seems quite simple and obvious. (We need to note that this is exactly the opposite of the objection that psychology is often common sense, as discussed in Section 20. But different people can have different objections, and we all frequently hold contradictory opinions at the same time without realizing it.)

One example of how psychologists seem to talk nonsense is the way we deal with the topic of aggression. To many people, it is obvious that people have aggressive instincts that build up until they must be released. The image of someone going home from a bad day at work and taking his aggression out on by kicking the cat or fighting with the family is a familiar one. We say we need to "get it out of our system."

The instinct view of aggression is very common, and it is shared at least in part by Aristotle, Sigmund Freud, Konrad Lorenz, and Ann Landers, among other prominent thinkers. According to Freud and Lorenz, people have aggressive instincts that constantly build up like pressure in a boiler and must be released one way or another. The preferred way is through a harmless substitute activity, variously known as *catharsis*, redirection, venting, or simply "letting off steam." Thus sports, theater, kicking the cat, and hitting your partner with a large, soft bat are supposed to be substitutes for war, spouse abuse, and the like. You can see why the instinct view is sometimes called the hydraulic model. The cathartic activities drain off the pressure before the system explodes.

This theory has a great deal of intuitive appeal. The only problem is, the situation is much more complicated. We will mention only a few of the problems. In the first place, there is little evidence that aggressive tendencies build up naturally over time. (This is the heart of the hydraulic theory.) People deprived of the opportunity to act aggressively don't become more and more nasty.

Second, the idea that releasing aggressive tendencies harmlessly results in catharsis is much in doubt. Considerable evidence exists that acting aggressively or even watching aggression can, under particular circumstances, actually increase aggression. Consider the riots that often break out in connection with sports events in many countries. To take a personal example, when someone cuts me off in traffic I get annoyed, as many people do. I have noticed that if I express my anger via aggressive words, gestures, or actions, it makes me even more angry than if I keep my thoughts to myself.

Research shows that under some conditions expressing aggressive thoughts is cathartic and under others it actually increases aggression. The situation is rather complicated, and not completely understood. But that is precisely my point. There is considerable evidence that aggression is caused by external provocation, such as threats and frustrations, not internally produced instincts. There is also evidence that people learn to act aggressively from watching other people and from finding out that it often permits them to get their way. And so forth. Any introductory psychology book will have a discussion of the ins and outs of aggression. It is a complicated subject, as are so many things psychology deals with.

At first glance, the psychologist seems to be talking nonsense. But when all things are considered, it begins to make sense, even if it isn't as simple as we would like it to be.

Exercise: Remember something you used to have a strong opinion on that eventually you came to understand was more complicated than you thought at the time.

Section 45

I Can't Buy Sociobiology Because It Justifies Polygamy

Principle: *To draw a value judgment from a scientific theory or data is to commit the naturalistic fallacy, to confuse "is" with "ought."*

Sociobiology is a relatively new branch of science that seeks to understand social behavior from an evolutionary viewpoint. A key idea of sociobiology is that behavior that increases an organism's chances of passing on its genes to the next generation will be favored by natural selection and sexual selection. One of the areas of interest to sociobiologists is that of reproductive strategies. Consider human reproduction. Men and women differ greatly in the investment necessary to produce offspring. At a minimum, men need only to contribute a small amount of sperm, which requires little behavioral or physiological investment. Females, on the other hand, produce relatively few eggs, and they must invest enormous energy into pregnancy, lactation, and nurturing to produce offspring.

These biological differences lead to different mating strategies between men and women. Because of his small investment in producing sperm, the optimal strategy for the male is to impregnate as many females as possible and to prefer females that appear likely to be the most fertile. The female, on the other hand, must be very choosy about which males she accepts, preferring males who give evidence that they will support their offspring.

Sociobiological thinking predicts a number of behavioral findings, such that men tend to be more promiscuous than women, and prefer younger women. Students frequently object to these implications of sociobiology, because they appear to justify behavior that is immoral, unethical, or at least politically incorrect.

Now it is true that sociobiology predicts that men will tend to be more promiscuous than women but it is not true that sociobiology justifies this fact. To go from predicting promiscuity to justifying it is to commit the *naturalistic fallacy*. In a nutshell, the naturalistic fallacy consists in arguing from "is" to "ought," from facts to value judgments (Taylor, 1975).

Take a few simple examples: Evolutionary theory predicts that parasites will make us sick, weeds will tend to crowd out crops, mice will eat stored corn, termites will destroy houses, and so on. Nevertheless, we have no ethical problems whatsoever in trying to eradicate disease and pestilence.

The naturalistic fallacy is very widespread. We have a strong tendency to assume that "is" means "ought." James Friedrich (1989) did an experiment in which subjects read the results of a number of studies, which found, for example, that advertising affected children's consumption of junk food. Later, the subjects tended to agree that the research found that advertising of junk food to children ought to be restricted, whereas no such conclusion had been present in the descriptions they had read of the research.

> **Exercise:** Show how the naturalistic fallacy could cause misuse of surveys of sexual behavior, cheating on income taxes, and the like.

Section 46

I Can't Buy Sociobiology Because Most of the Time We Aren't Trying to Pass on Our Genes

Principle: *Causes of behavior do not always operate at the level of consciousness.*

This question arose when I was explaining that sociobiology predicts that men will tend to choose women whose appearance suggests they will be likely to bear children, and women will prefer men who appear likely to support children. The objection was that most of the time people aren't trying to mate and pass on their genes, as sociobiology predicts; they are just dating, socializing, or whatever.

We can grant that people consciously think about passing on their genes much less frequently than they think about having fun, meeting interesting people, and the like. But sociobiology is not limited to predicting mating behavior per se; it predicts what attributes people will find attractive in others. These attributes will influence choice of partners for dates and how we act in many other social situations.

The misconception that my questioner seemed to be operating under was that causes of behavior must operate at the level of consciousness—that we must be aware of why we are doing something like flirting with an attractive person. It is true that we often are aware of why we do something, or assume that we ought to be. You may have had the experience of going into your bedroom to get an item of clothing that needed to be laundered and then forgetting why you went there. You may have stopped, scratched your head, and said, "Now, why did I come here?—Oh, yeah, I need to wash that shirt!"

Many theories of psychology give an important role to awareness in explaining behavior, and properly so. Attribution theory, for example, which was discussed in Section 43 and is probably discussed in your textbook, concerns how we consciously think about the causes of people's behavior. No problem.

But at least since the time of Freud we have known that we are often not consciously aware of why we do things. Examples abound, but Freudian slips are familiar to us all. The fact is that a great deal of our cognitive processes takes place at a level that is completely unavailable to consciousness. For example, we have no idea at all how we go about remembering something, such as our mother's maiden name, or the words to the "The Star Spangled Banner." Things just pop into our awareness when we remember them (if we do). As far as sociobiology is concerned, it simply predicts what characteristics of the opposite sex we will find attractive. It says nothing about our conscious thoughts concerning these choices.

The reasons for our preferences will often be completely mysterious to us. We may be able to describe the features of an attractive person in great, loving detail. But we will be at a complete loss to say why those features should fascinate us so much. If we try, we will just start going in circles: He's cute because he has such wavy hair. What's so great about wavy hair? Well, because wavy hair is nice. The fact is, we have no direct insight into why these things appeal to us. They just do.

> **Exercise:** Look in the chapter on social psychology in your textbook and find two theories that deal with behavior at the level of conscious awareness. Then find two that do not assume awareness.

References

AMERICAN LAW INSTITUTE. (1985). *Model Penal Code.* Philadelphia, PA: Author.

BEM, D, J., & HONORTON, C. (1994). Does Psi exist? Replicable evidence for an anomalous process of information transfer. *Psychological Bulletin, 115,* 4–18.

BLAU, G. L., McGINLEY, H., & PASEWARK, R. (1993). Understanding the use of the insanity defense. *Journal of Clinical Psychology, 49,* 435–440.

BOK, B. J., & JEROME, L. E. (1975). *Objections to astronomy.* Buffalo, NY: Prometheus Books. (Also published in *The Humanist, 35,*(5). 1975.)

BROOKFIELD, S. D. (1987). *Developing critical thinkers: Challenging adults to explore alternative ways of thinking and acting.* San Francisco: Jossey–Bass.

BUSCAGLIA, L. (1992). *Born for Love.* New York: Ballantine.

CEDERBLOM, J., & PAULSEN, D. W. (1986). *Critical reasoning* (2nd ed.). Belmont, CA: Wadsworth.

COLLINGS, V. B. (1974). Human taste response as a function of locus of stimulation on the tongue and soft palate. *Perception and Psychophysics, 16,* 169–174.

DIACONIS, P. & MOSTELLER, F. (1989). Methods for studying coincidences. *Journal of the American Statistical Association, 84,* 853–861.

ELLIS, A. (1993). The advantages and disadvantages of self-help therapy materials. *Professional Psychology: Research and Practice, 24,* 335–339.

FOREWARD, S. & BUCK, C. (1992). *Obsessive love: When it hurts too much to let go.* New York: Bantam.

FRIEDRICH, J. (1989). Drawing moral inferences from descriptive science: The impact of attitudes on naturalistic fallacy errors. *Personality and Social Psychology Bulletin, 15,* 414–425.

GARDNER, M. (1976). *The incredible Dr. Matrix.* New York: Scribners.

GARDNER, M. (1981). *Science: good, bad, and bogus.* Buffalo, NY: Prometheus.

GERGEN, K. G. (1994). Exploring the postmodern: Perils or potentials? *American Psychologist, 49,* 412–416.

GROSS, P. R., & LEVITT, N. (1994). *Higher superstition: The academic left and its quarrels with science.* Baltimore: Johns Hopkins University Press.

HEFFERLINE, R. F., KEENAN, B., & HARFORD, R. A. (1959). Escape and avoidance conditioning in human subjects without their observation of the response. *Science, 130,* 1338–1339.

HERGENHAHN, B. R. (1992). *An introduction to the history of psychology* (2nd ed.). Belmont, CA: Wadsworth.

HINES, T. M. (1979). Biorhythm theory: A critical review. *The Skeptical Inquirer, 3*(4), 26–36.

KEY, W. B. (1973). *Subliminal seduction.* Englewood Cliffs, NJ: Prentice-Hall.

MACMILLAN, M. B. (1986). A wonderful journey through skull and brains: The travels of Mr. Gage's tamping iron. *Brain and Cognition, 5,* 67–107.

MCPECK, J. E. (1990). *Teaching critical thinking: Dialogue and dialectic.* New York: Routledge.

MOOK, D. G. (1983). In defense of external invalidity. *American Psychologist, 38,* 379–387.

MYERS, D. (1992/1995). *Psychology* (3rd ed./4th ed.). New York: Worth.

NISBETT, R. E., BORGIDA, E., CRANDALL, R., & REED, H. (1976). Popular induction: Information is not necessarily informative. In J. S. Carroll and J. W. Payne (Eds.), *Cognition and social behavior.* Hillsdale, NJ: Erlbaum.

PALFREMEN, J. (Director). (1993). Prisoners of silence. *Frontline* (FROL202). PBS Video. Boston: WGBH Educational Foundation.

PAUL, R. W., & NOSICH, G. M. (1991). *A proposal for the national assessment of higher-order thinking at the community college, college, and university levels.* Washington, DC: National Center for Education Statistics. U.S. Department of Education.

PECK, M. S. (1978). *The road less traveled: A new psychology of love, traditional values, and spiritual growth.* New York: Simon & Schuster.

PUTHOFF, H. E., & TARG, R. (1974). Information transfer under conditions of sensory shielding. *Nature, 252,* 602–607.

RESNICK, L. B. (1987). *Education and learning to think.* Washington, DC: National Academy Press.

ROGERS, S. (1992–1993). How a publicity blitz created the myth of subliminal advertising. *Public Relations Quarterly,* (Winter), 12–17.

Ross, L. D. (1977). The intuitive psychologist and his shortcomings: Distortions in the attribution process. In L. Berkowitz (Ed.), *Advances in experimental social psychology* (Vol. 10). New York: Academic Press.

Sardello, R. (1994). *Facing the world with soul.* New York: Harper/Collins.

Schaffner, P. E. (1985). Specious learning about reward and punishment. *Journal of Personality and Social Psychology, 48,* 1377–1388.

Scott, J. P., & Fuller, J. L. (1974). *Dog behavior: The genetic basis.* Chicago: University of Chicago Press.

Seger, C. A. (1994). Implicit learning. *Psychological Bulletin, 115,* 163–196.

Slovic, P., & Fischoff, B. (1977). On the psychology of experimental surprises. *Journal of Experimental Psychology: Human Perception and Performance, 3,* 544–551.

Sno, H. N., & Linszen, D. H. (1990). The déjà vu experience: remembrance of things past? *American Journal of Psychiatry, 147,* 1587–1595.

Taylor, P. W. (1975). *Principles of ethics: An introduction.* Encino, CA: Dickenson.

Van Fleet, J. K. (1994). *The power within! Tap your inner force and program yourself for success.* Englewood Cliffs, NJ: Prentice-Hall.

Vokey, J. R., & Read, J. D. (1985). Subliminal messages: Between the Devil and the media. *American Psychologist, 40,* 1231–1239.

Wever, R. A. (1979). *The circadian system of man.* New York: Springer-Verlag.

World almanac and book of facts. (1994). New York: Press Publishing.

List of Principles by Key Words

Answerable, science deals with questions that are (Section 41)

Artificial situations provide opportunity to study phenomena in purest form (Section 29)

Belief in theory based on data, not personal preference (Section 3)

Beliefs contradicted by science, everyone's (Section 7)

Beliefs often held because of their usefulness (Section 18)

Biology can provide insights into behavior (Section 13)

Burden of proof on those who make claim (Section 23)

Coincidence, to be considered as, events must first be noticed (Section 31)

Common sense differs from time to time and is shaped by psychological research (Section 20)

Complicated, nature is more c. than any one theory (Section 35)

Consciousness, causes of behavior often do not operate at the level of (Section 46)

Confuse "is" with "ought" is to commit naturalistic fallacy (Section 45)

Counterintuitive, complicated answer often correct (Section 44)

Documentation, importance of (Section 10)

Emergent properties of organisms, many behaviors are (Section 14)

Essentialism is philosophical error of trying to find what something really is (Section 16)

"Everyone knows" many things that aren't true (Section 11)

Fundamental attribution error leads to underestimating importance of situation (Section 43)